THE "FORBIDDEN" SECRETS OF A ONE MAN EMPIRE

THE "FORBIDDEN" SECRETS OF A ONE MAN EMPIRE

12 Controversial, Real World and Independently Verified IRON LAWS for the Self-Made Man Who Wants to Radically Make More Money, Have More Freedom and Be More Man, Even in the New Economy and Without Being Overwhelmed, Overstretched, Fatigued or Panicked.

Published By OME Global Ltd. One Man Empire is a trademark of OME Global Ltd. www.theonemanempire.com

ISBN 9798713954253

Interior illustrations: Lucas Viso

Disclaimer

The author of this book does not dispense business advice, only offers information of a general nature to help you in your quest for business success. This book is not designed to be a definitive guide or to take the place of advice from a qualified professional, and there is no guarantee that the methods suggested in this book will be successful, owing to the risk that is involved in business of almost any kind. Thus, neither the publisher nor the author assume liability for any losses that may be sustained by the use of the methods described in this book, and any such liability is hereby expressly disclaimed. In the event you use any of the information in this book for yourself, the author and the publisher assume no responsibility for your actions.

THE "FORBIDDEN" SECRETS OF A ONE MAN EMPIRE

12 Controversial, Real World and Independently Verified IRON LAWS for the Self-Made Man Who Wants to Radically Make More Money, Have More Freedom and Be More Man, Even in the New Economy and Without Being Overwhelmed, Overstretched, Fatigued or Panicked

CHARLIE HUTTON

DEDICATION

To Brad "I Don't Give A Fuck" Johnson, the original One Man
Empire and man responsible for igniting my passion for operating
at the helm of the business. I'm so grateful that you took the time
to inspire (brainwash) a young, green, "English wanker" with stories
about what it really takes to stand on your own two feet.

TABLE OF CONTENTS

Part 3. The Universal Iron Laws of Freedom

INTRODUCTION

Your Baptism of Fire

OK, my friend. First things first, let me congratulate you on stepping up and deciding to purchase this book. The truth is – and if those that have read these pages before you are a measuring stick – this one simple decision to double down and invest in yourself shows me you are the kind of man that has the guts and determination to stand on his own two feet. A dedicated, dynamic individual with a strong intuition and a thirst for something more.

As you are about to discover, the 12 Iron Laws in this book are the backbone for the most successful men that are walking the face of the earth TODAY. Consider them the NEW code of conduct for the NEW breed of self-made man to start operating from the ground up, to provide and protect.

In fact, if you look you will see hard evidence of these laws in play in the lives of Genghis Khan, Napoleon, Caesar, Churchill, Lincoln, Carnegie, Ford, Edison, Rockefeller, Jobs, Musk,

Disney, Zuckerberg and Bezos to name just a few. Each rose to power with an understanding of the spoils that await those who choose to leverage these "forbidden" secrets to radically make more, provide more and be more.

The laws you are about to uncover are a refinement of the concepts I've formalised on stage and around the world in front of the most misunderstood and underappreciated group in society today: the male business owner and entrepreneur.

After the explosive, underground One Man Empire docu-series took the male business owner community by storm – racking up close to 3.21 million views in a few short weeks – it became clear this book was needed, a scripture in the form of the fundamental IRON LAWS governing what it takes to successfully become a One Man Empire in today's fucked up blur of boom or bust:

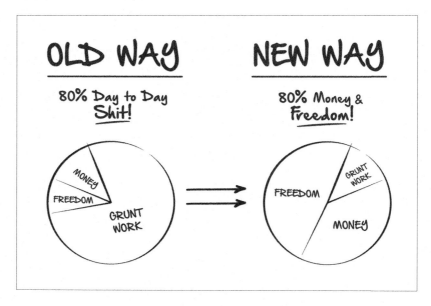

Truth is, the men who have already made the decision to adopt these principles have started to see results like this:

This is the tip of the iceberg of what you can expect from the next 200 pages of this book, and its three fundamental parts.

PART 1. THE IRON LAWS OF *MAN*

The fundamental laws needed to develop a stone-cold, unshakeable CONFIDENCE as the most powerful **MAN** in any room, any environment and any situation without getting nervous, fearful or caught in the act. Or, in other words, the art and science of rapidly increasing loyalty and respect from others.

PART 2. THE IRON LAWS OF *MONEY*

The unwritten laws of wealth attraction for the self-made man to CONSISTENTLY and effortlessly attract more **MONEY**. What some would call an instant shot in the arm to any man of value who wants to radically stack the deck of status and standing in his favour.

PART 3. THE IRON LAWS OF *FREEDOM*

The forbidden secret to real CONTROL. How to unlock the potential in your operation, so that no matter where you are in the world, no matter what you are doing and who you are doing it with, you have 100% **FREEDOM**, because things are moving predictably and like clockwork.

… Everything I suspect that you got into this game for, in the first place.

If you are just getting your business off the ground, if you are doing up to $150K in sales before your first full-time employee, if you are making $150K-$1m in revenue with a small team, or if you are already doing over $1m in revenue and looking to scale faster you, my friend, are in good company and in the right place.

So, as you start to imagine finally being free from the confusion, free from the chaos and free from the invisible chains that have kept you a prisoner inside your own business from day dot, and before you start to see yourself waking up each and every morning with TOTAL CONFIDENCE, TOTAL CONSISTENCY & TOTAL CONTROL, I first must issue you with:

A Stark Word of Warning

Even though you may have seen me on stage, watched me on TV or heard some of my controversy on the radio or online,

4

I must make it clear that I will not sugar-coat the life we lead or this path that we have chosen.

IF YOU ARE EASILY OFFENDED AND WANT SOMEONE TO BEAT AROUND THE BUSH – I SUGGEST YOU DO NOT CARRY ON

Despite everything you're about to uncover being battle-tested by countless men, in countless industries and in countless countries, I ask that you continue with an open mind.

You see we are all born the same. Free from any preconceived limitations around the order of man in today's game.

Trouble is, eventually, most of us submit to the rules of what others in society demand, forcing our natural-born impulses towards comfort, compliance and blame.

It's how most end up settling. Mediocrity becomes the new normal.

So as you begin you must consider clearing your head of the preconceptions you have around operating as a man at the helm of a business.

What You're About to Uncover Here Are Radical Concepts

Iron Laws of Man, Iron Laws of Money and Iron Laws of Freedom that will challenge your perspective on you, others and what you deem is possible as just one man at the helm of a business.

Truth is, at first you will violently disagree with some of these laws. Others will finally allow the penny to drop. Some will challenge your beliefs around what is fair and how we ought to do business, while others will rubber-stamp experiences and situations you have faced first-hand.

Some are ugly, some are controversial, some are not politically correct.

Yet in the Cold Hard Light of Day, Each Is a Universally Verified Truth

It's exactly why from this page and moving forward, I want you to make it your moral obligation to study every word of every law with an open mind. For those that choose to read this book and take responsibility to apply what they discover with speed and full force, ahead lies the power to continue something great.

So let me assure you of this:

➜ **If you've ever felt an ounce of guilt, remorse or unrest in your current situation and your business...**

➜ **If you've ever felt ready to rid yourself of the overwhelm, the fatigue and the panic that's all too common in this game...**

➜ **If you've ever felt sick to the back teeth of working your arse off just to stand still – or worse, go backwards...**

Then, right here, inside this book, is where those who are gasping for air finally breathe. Those that have plateaued make a fundamental shift towards the light. And those struggling in a never-ending spiral of feast and famine rise up in a blaze of glory and are born free.

If you are ready to begin, then turn the page to start your baptism of fire, because by the time you're done you won't recognise the man you've become, the business you operate, or the life that you lead. And neither will anyone else.

Make More. Provide More. Be More.
Charlie "I Am A One Man Empire" Hutton

READ FIRST

How to Profit From This Book

What most smart self-made men understand is that rich people have BIG LIBRARIES and SMALL TVs.

It's why – like Bezos, Branson and Buffet – I make it part of my personal code of conduct to read one, two or sometimes even three books a week.

Now I suspect by the very fact that you've picked this publication off the shelf, you also understand the power of the knowledge that comes in the written word. However, if you've tried to get your shit in order before by leveraging books, and failed, then I'll have you consider it's not your fault.

Chances are it's because of what we're taught in school about reading and consuming information. Because here's the thing about information – it's just that. Information. In one ear and out the other.

And herein lies the problem with reading for the sake of gathering information. Information is just words on a page unless you approach it with a STRATEGY to DEPLOY it and make it work for you.

Which is why right now I want you to understand how to best approach the Iron Laws in this book:

1. **Glance through each law at a high level to start with. Read the headlines and highlights so you get a good overview of what is at stake.**

2. **Stop yourself from getting distracted by the details at first. Some ideas may seem hard or tough when you start. Most are neither. You will come away with a set of simple instructions and a clear way forward.**

3. The ideas in this book come from a wealth of experience acquired through a lot of mistakes costing a great deal of money and emotional heartache. That said, you may find that you don't share every experience, so remember you must keep an eye on the BIG picture.

4. Stop your initial emotional responses getting in the way of common sense and first-hand experience.

5. Don't carry on past this next page if you are the type of person who starts but does not finish. You must decide to start this process and be present and persistent with it to the end.

6. Be prepared to buck the trend on conventional ways of thinking about business, family and life, that many have been subject to, and stuck with, from an early age.

7. Be open to new ways of operating that will transform money, wealth, status, respect and power to levels that most men have never considered possible.

8. Be ready to accept FULL responsibility for your actions. Only you can do this. Only you can make a shift. The choice is yours and the time is now.

9. Remember, life is short. Don't let the opportunity pass.

How to Profit from Others in This Book

In this book you will hear, first-hand, "Tales From The Trenches" of other men, in other businesses, that have already started to put these laws into action. Revelations, results and rewards all laid bare and in plain sight ready for you to see, copy and deploy.

Which means you must fully understand the word "business".

Just one word on the surface, but there are so many types, so many industries, so many products and so many services. Meaning you could make the assumption that no two businesses are ever the same.

This is a dangerous assumption to have.

Understand that when you rip the guts out, just as all men bleed the same, all businesses make money the same. By selling. By fulfilling what was promised. And by creating happy customers on the back of that fulfilment.

It's why in this book and in any environment, the lessons learnt from other men, in other businesses, in other industries are universal – no matter how irrelevant, inapplicable, or stupid they might seem at first glance.

Universal laws, just like gravity and physics. Applicable no matter your situation. Man or mouse. Black or white. Big or small. You just need to open your eyes and see the similarities.

Once you start connecting the dots and the mess that's in your head, an almighty force will emerge – the complete picture, an understanding that will guarantee you move the dial.

The only question you need to ask is this:

How COULD I leverage what these other successful men are doing, in MY business?

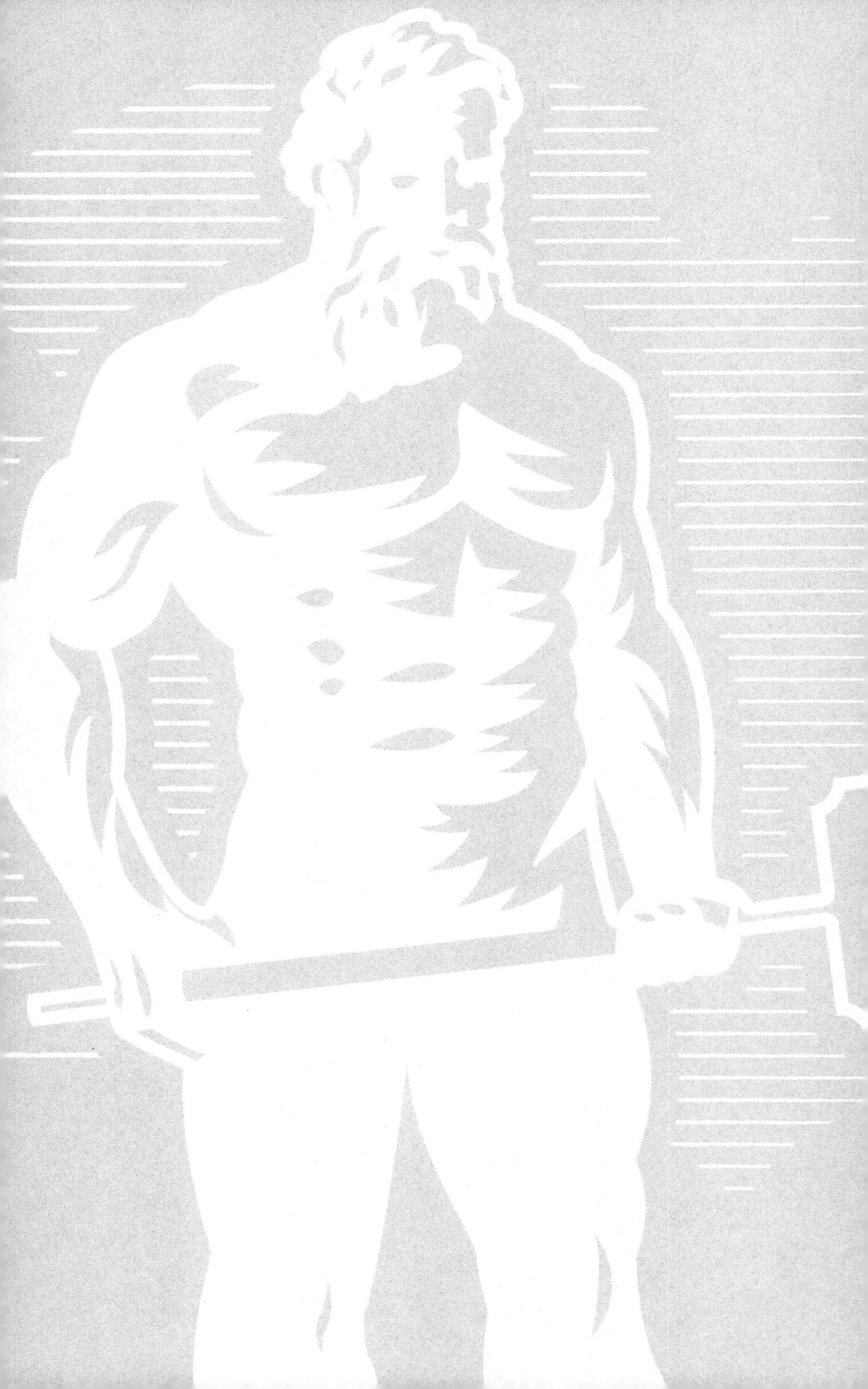

PART 1

THE UNIVERSAL IRON LAWS OF
MAN

"Courage Is Being Scared To Death And Saddling Up Anyway"
- John Wayne

IRON LAW #1

Relentlessly Resist Being Overstretched, To Prevent Being Royally Fucked

It's July 17th, 2013 and I'm alone.

Mentally that is – not physically.

It's Thursday morning. I'm in the kitchen, my bags have been packed and I'm sat opposite my wife Emma and my four-day-old son Barney. Emma won't talk to me and I can't say I blame her. Still, I thought I'd done the right thing by going.

You see, two days earlier and less than 48 hours after our son was born, I was driving up the M6 to see a client. And as it turns out, that apparently makes me a selfish prick, EVEN if I'm doing it to keep the money coming in and the business a success.

Trouble is, there's only so much selfishness, suffering and sacrifice the people around us can take. And that Thursday morning, as I ate my breakfast staring at the packed bags in the hallway, I knew this was it. I knew I was in too deep.

It's a dark place, and one that I'd begun to call No Man's Land after being at the helm of my own business for the last eight years – a never-ending shit show of complete and utter conflict and crisis, that always started with a trigger.

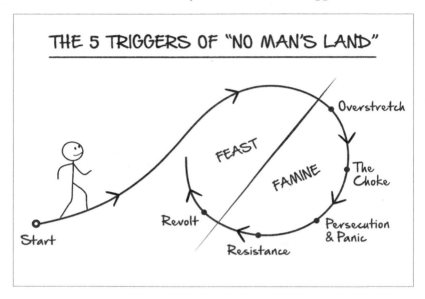

Trigger #1: Overstretch

Whatever the cause, the fallout is simple enough. A state that's simply down to our male primal instinct to **provide more**. A raw desire to take on more work and more business than we should. A desire that is all too often amplified by a willingness to please others by saying YES.

→   YES to things because we feel we have to.

→   YES to things that deep down we know we

shouldn't.

→ And YES to things that in the cold hard light of day often cause more harm than good.

Now, I'll have you consider, the BIG problem with reaching overstretch is that for most it immediately leads to trigger number two:

Trigger #2: The Choke

I suspect you've already experienced the pain of The Choke first-hand. Because The Choke is that place when you're still awake at 2.37 a.m. and you're like, "FUCK!"

→ FUCK I've still got emails to do...

→ FUCK I've still got quotes to follow up...

→ FUCK I've still got customers to deal with...

→ FUCK I've got a family that deserves my time...

→ And FUCK I don't have the time to do all of it...

And herein lies the big problem with The Choke –

something has to give. And when something has to give, the lowest hanging fruit falls from the tree and stops you dead in your tracks:

→ Sales stop.

→ Marketing stops.

→ Family stops.

It's exactly why, during The Choke, we ALWAYS hit trigger number three.

Trigger #3: Persecution & Panic

Understand that the definition of persecution is hostility and ill-treatment towards those of differing beliefs.

Now, for us that play this game, it means:

→ Persecution from customers for dragging our feet...

→ Persecution from prospects because we've not returned calls...

→ And, most importantly, persecution from spouses or partners because we're never 100% present.

And I get it. Persecution is not fair.

Because, when push comes to shove, it's not our fault.

I mean, after all, we're just trying to do the right thing – provide and protect, and that sometimes means sacrifices.

Trouble is, those sacrifices – and our internal justification of WHY they're OK – don't fix the guilt.

They don't stop the arguments at home, and they don't buy you back time.

It's EXACTLY why, in my experience, persecution drags most to the bottom of the barrel. A place of even longer workdays, sleepless nights and more suffering. One that leaves us more frustrated, fatigued and PANICKED as our bodies suffer both mentally and physically.

Now here's the thing. When you hit that place, there are two ways to go. Collapse and fail. OR suck it up and suffer in silence.

Trigger #4: Persistence

Those that fight on face a period of hustle – nose to the grindstone in the distant hope that you can fight your way out of this misery by just working harder and getting shit done.

Because that's what men are supposed to do, right?

Complete and utter persistence in one thing, and one thing only – WORK.

Work justified to those around us by the belief that everything will be OK if we can just:

➜   Get that next thing ticked off the list.

➜   Get that customer of our back.

➜ **Make that next sale.**

Now the funny thing is, if you persistently work for long and hard enough, the odds will tell you that things will turn around and you will trigger a Revolt.

Trigger #5: Revolt

Somewhere on the surface, that seems like a good place. One where you can finally breathe a sigh of relief because you can see the wood through the trees and finally start focusing on making money again.

But here's the kicker.

I'll have you consider that when you fight your way through No Man's Land with pure male aggression, hard work and persistence there's only one way in which it can go.

Sometimes, it's only a matter of weeks, other times it takes months, sometimes years.

BUT one thing is certain. A REVOLT by its nature will always be followed by crisis and conflict, and crisis and conflict is always followed by overstretch.

It's why FEAST AND FAMINE is so prevalent...

It's why no business, in no sector, is immune....

It's why the divorce rate for the likes of you and I at the helm of a business is so high.

And before you say it:

Getting More Customers Is Not the Answer

You see, there is a funny thing that happens when you scale.

Customers come to only want to deal with you (the man at the top) because they feel anyone else in the business isn't quite up to scratch. So y-o-u end up being the one with his fingers in all the pies. The one doing all the calls. The one copied in on all the emails. And the one handling all the fallout (usually at the weekend or out-of-hours) – even if you have employees on the ground and in the business.

Meaning the lion's share of the work sits with one man, the very same man that in most circumstances is already on his knees and at the end of his tether.

It's why most employee-up, in one last-ditch attempt to keep growing and break the deadlock.

The trouble is...

More Employees Accelerate Overstretch – They Don't Fix It

Here's what people don't realise when their back's against the wall and they're under the cosh. These kinds of employee hires get made out of necessity, and not strategy. And when you hire out of necessity, I'll have you consider most never pick the right people for the job.

Most choose competence over character. And here's the problem with competent employees, they are just that – competent. Nothing more, nothing less:

→ They're not punctual.

→ They always make excuses.

→ They do the bare minimum and have no drive.

→ They think they're smarter than you.

→ They don't believe in your business or you.

→ They're constantly making demands.

→ They don't get along with anyone.

The net result being, rather than reducing overstretch, more employees (and more customers) amplify it.

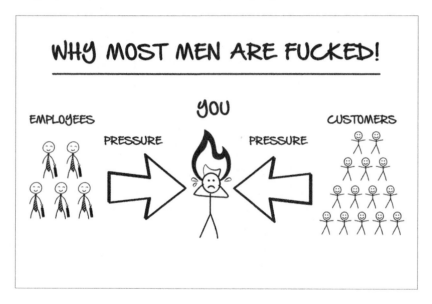

You Become the Bottleneck and You Become Overstretched

It's the very reason that most plateau and most can never profitably scale – simply because it becomes physically impossible to handle any more without it all collapsing like a house of cards.

This begs the question, is it any wonder the thought of taking a holiday is so fucking scary because you're nothing more than piggy in the middle?

Now here's the thing you need to see. When you start out it's OK to look for MORE and it's OK for you to be the centre of your universe. BUT if you don't adapt as you grow, then it's YOU that becomes the breaking point, bottleneck and the noose around your own neck.

THE REVELATION FROM THE LAW

Overstretch is the catalyst, and it kills all momentum, marriages and money.

Frankly, by its symptoms, a man that is Overstretched can never be free, no matter how much success it looks like he has on the outside.

It's why your number one goal must revolve around being able to spot Overstretch before it starts, and stop it dead in its tracks. From my experience with those that have made this journey before, below are a few of the tell-tell signs that Overstretch is imminent:

1. **Long wait times.** Work is delayed because people are waiting on you for information, or next actions.

2. **Backlog of work.** There's too much work-in, and not enough time to push it out.

3. **High stress levels.** A feeling of being attacked on all sides and pulled in every direction.

The Good News

The good news is, now that you know exactly why most men in this game are fucked, the focus of the rest of the Iron Laws in this book will be directed at what you need to do to finally pull yourself kicking and screaming out of No Man's Land and take back control for good.

IRON LAW #2

Live By A Code Or Die By Your Own Desires

True story...

At the age of 18, I packed up, shipped out and moved to Vancouver, Canada – on my own.

Young, dumb and stupid, I fell under the wing of an unusually astute businessman. A guiding light for my personal journey and a man that I came to know as Brad "I Don't Give A Fuck" Johnson.

I'll explain the nickname later, but for now I need you to understand that there was nothing special about this man when we first met.

He drove an old Dodge pickup truck with bullet holes in the side. He was dressed down and ready for a hard day's work, in a checked flannel shirt, dusty denim jeans and cowboy boots. If you met him in the street you wouldn't look twice. He'd been to jail and worked with his hands all his life.

On the face of it, he was just another average man, running another average business.

Yet, he was one of the smartest and most exceptional businessmen that I have ever had the pleasure to meet and call "family".

Everywhere we went, people wanted to speak to him. And when he spoke, everyone listened. His crew were loyal and gave him full credit for turning their lives around. Customers respected his opinion and happily paid him double the going rate. His business card simply said, "I'll call you!"

In the evenings and at weekends he was family-focused – doing as he chose, when he chose to do it. And good luck? Well, that seemed to be magnetically attracted to him, wherever he was, and in whatever he would do.

This Man Truly Had It All:

→ Money

→ Family

→ Respect

→ Loyalty

→ Opportunity

→ Freedom

What was the secret that allowed this normal man to truly make more, provide more and be more than most?

The same vital ingredient that has been the making of the self-made man since the dawn of time:

By Starting to Control Daily Standards

You see, the definition of a standard is this:

> noun
>
> **A principle of conduct informed by notions of honour and decency.**
> *"He had high moral standards"*

It was the first question Brad asked me after Emma had packed my bags and kicked me out on my ear:

"Are You Holding Yourself to High Enough Standards?"

Well the truth is, I wasn't.

My discipline was all to shit, and my standards were all out of whack.

Now here's what most don't understand. Men like you and I have the power to mould the mind and create a conscious catalyst that will FORCE us to push further than we ever thought possible.

Because the truth is, it's the thoughts that run through the minds of men that determine if they win or lose. Trouble is, far too many men on this journey forget the mental discipline it takes to stay in control. A subtle mental shift, that forces focus to a destructive declaration of goals instead of success-oriented standards.

Desire-driven goals are important and do push men forward but now, more than ever, you need to consider that goals can and will collapse like a house of cards.

If the COVID-19 pandemic has shown us anything, it's that goals can be terminated overnight and without warning. The reality being – for the first time ever – that your business could be mandated to shut its doors and batten down its hatches, or face the full wrath of the law.

➔   **Targets missed.**

➔   **Dreams shattered.**

➔   **Goals crushed.**

The fact is, goals only ever remind you of the shit you haven't got done. It's why most goals only ever trigger overwhelm, instead of removing it.

Standards Not Goals Will Always Be Making a Man

Your standards are your code of conduct, the things that you hold accountable to you. They are your code of honour. They are your own internal force of nature that you keep moving forward.

They are the disciplines and behaviours, as a man, you consistently act out, to allow you to provide and protect – NO MATTER WHAT.

➔   **Hitting $50K this month – that's a goal.**

→ Deciding to make 50 calls a day, every day – that's a standard.

→ Dropping 20lbs – that's a goal.

→ Deciding to hit the weights for 20 minutes a day, every day – that's a standard.

Improving relationships at home – that's a goal.

Choosing to switch off the fucking phone at 5 p.m. every day – that's a standard.

One is about hoping, the other is about discipline.

One can be sabotaged by other people, the other is something you demand of yourself.

Now a wise man once said:

"Knowing What You Will Stand for Is More Important, Than Knowing What You Won't…"

It's why I urge you as you start on this journey to start swapping personal goals for personal standards.

That means:

1. Getting Clear on Your Current Situation

Understanding how your current day-to-day behaviours are determining your actions and your results.

2. Getting Clear on Your Current Objectives

Truth is, it's impossible to raise your standards if you don't know what it is that you want.

3. Getting Clear on Your New Daily Code of Conduct

Defining the standards you need to operate by in order to hit your current objectives. This list will become your NEW code of conduct and what you must hold yourself accountable to each and every day.

The 7 Universal Operating Standards of a One Man Empire

1.   I am a One Man Empire because every day I will accept full responsibility for myself and the choices

I make. There are no such things as excuses, only choices. And choices are a privilege that I must earn every day.

2. I am a One Man Empire because every day I will never quit and will do whatever it takes. I understand that to provide for my family, I need to physically work harder and be mentally stronger than my mediocre male counterparts.

3. I am a One Man Empire because every day I will be open to new ideas and take criticism like a man. I fully understand that the answers I WANT to hear and the answers I NEED to hear are likely to be two completely different things.

4. I am a One Man Empire because every day I will act with speed and decision, and in a manner as if my life and the lives of my family depend on it.

5. I am a One Man Empire because every day total commitment will be my constant companion and personal integrity will be my mentor.

6. I am a One Man Empire because every day I will have the discipline to persevere in the midst of obstacles, and fight on in the face of defeat; avoiding the temptation of shortcuts that can lead to disappointment, and unhealthy habits that can

result in defeat.

7. I am a One Man Empire because I approach every day with 100% confidence in what I do and how I operate.

THE REVELATION FROM THE LAW

Standards are the measuring stick for daily life as a man at the helm of a business today. They should be built on a foundation of:

➜ Modesty

➜ Sanity

➜ Simplicity

Because in my experience:

➜ No man is more alone than the man trying to please everyone other than himself.

➜ No man is more overstretched than the man trying to do everything by himself.

➜ No man is more conflicted than the man trying to be everything to all men.

Understand that for the self-made man, this game is

meaningless if your standards have no meaning.

It's why the man who has total control, is always the man who:

→   Knows what he values.

→   Knows what he really wants.

→   And knows what he needs to do each day to get it.

Remember the success of any man will be always judged by his standards, never his goals.

IRON LAW #3

Contamination: Avoid The Weak-Willed & Weak-Minded.

I'm alone. I'm in the line at the post office and there are three people in front of me – one man, two ladies (and a dog) who all seem to be together and in one group. I say group, but based on what I could overhear, it was nothing short of a meeting of mediocrity.

The two ladies were divulging their thoughts on "the state of Lichfield", the small market town where I live. A cutting conversation that went along the lines of:

→ "Lichfield was going to the dogs."

→ "The local economy was going to the dogs."

→ "This country was going to the dogs."

However despite all of this, the two women in question had clearly chosen to stay put and stay in town, rather than choosing to get in a car, driving off, and going somewhere else. Something that I can only put down to a lack of mental metal, an inability to take control of their situation and do what needed to be done. A common trait of the weak-willed and the weak-minded; or what we in this environment call the rank and file mediocre majority.

The interesting fact being that you could put this type of person on the beach, in the Bahamas, with a cocktail in their hand and they would still bitch and moan.

The trouble being this specific type of person gets their power from putting others down. Operating like a dripping tap of doom and gloom that, given enough time, force feeds and infiltrates the mind of even the strongest man.

Like water torture or death by a hundred paper cuts, the contamination is slow but the diagnosis for those that entertain this type of company is always the same.

Mediocrity.

In fact, if you've come away from a conversation with someone, feeling down, depressed and in dire straits, the chances are this is the reason why.

Because, my friend, in my experience when the rubber hits the road then men like you and I must guard our minds, guard our senses and guard our environments with an iron fortress.

There are only so many hours in the day, and when push comes to shove, the self-made man does not have the luxury of being able to be side-tracked or side-swiped by those who would rather shit on you than succeed.

It's why I'd urge you right now to take heed of those who

you spend your most time with and look out for:

The 15 Warnings Signs of The Weak-Willed And The Weak-Minded

1. They are never wrong and it's never their fault.

2. They are not happy for you when you achieve something good in your life.

3. They prefer arguments. They must win the argument.

4. They love gossip, and they like to talk about others behind their backs.

5. Their life is full of drama and they drag you into it.

6. They love to take from you and find it hard to give you anything.

7. They belittle you to keep you under their control.

8. They manage to find the worst in every situation (even good ones).

9. They are never thankful for anything.

10. They don't apologise.

11. They revel in being the victim.

12. They are critical of others.

13. They make you feel defensive about your decisions.

14. They are inconsistent in their behaviour.

15. They boast about their achievements.

If any of these rings true for those you spend any considerable time with, it's vital to eradicate them from your environment quickly and with full force – before the contamination continues.

And by the way, this contamination is not restricted to just people.

The Mass Mediocre Are Only the Start of It

If the facts from Netflix's ground-breaking "Social Dilemma" documentary are to be believed, then men like you and I would be wise to be wary of cognitive contamination from:

→ Social platforms

→ Mainstream media

→ Political puppets

Their ability to deal in non-meaningful specifics, with words like "could", "might" and "maybe" sow seeds of doubt at every turn. Truth is, in my experience the mainstream media choose to underplay good economic news while overexaggerating the bad – or in other words, they have a habit of force-feeding fear. That is:

→ The fear of poverty.

→ The fear of criticism.

→ The fear of ill health.

→ The fear of love loss.

→ The fear of old age.

→ And the fear of death.

Six fundamental fears that do nothing but fuck with the minds of even the strongest self-made men by installing negative thoughts.

The trouble being that negative thoughts lead to negative acts, and negative acts lead to negative action. Negative action being nothing but procrastination through a fear of making a decision.

It's why...

You Must Protect Your Mind From All Intruders at *All* Costs

As this new economy emerges, only the strong-minded, self-made man will survive.

Weak will and negative thought in any form, and in any

media, is contagious, can have catastrophic consequences and should be avoided, eradicated and exterminated without a second look.

Case in point: Joe Harvie, founder and man at the helm of Scotland's fastest growing junk removal business. At the deepest, darkest point of his own personal No Man's Land, Joe identified his Facebook feed as the number one contributing factor to his infection from the inferior.

A daily morning ritual that had rapidly evolved into:

1.   Waking up.

2.   Hitting the can.

3.   Needing something to read.

4.   Opening Facebook.

5.   Quickly becoming drained by the derogatory damnation of the rank and file mediocre majority.

Meaning before the clock had even struck 8 a.m., Joe's mind (like so many others) had already been dragged through the gutter and sacrificed to the negative thoughts, feelings and fears of others.

Something he was smart enough to identify and eradicate with one fell swoop by deploying a new standard for his daily shit.

The switch from fear-fuelled Facebook, to success-based shorts. Or in other words, the deliberate reading about the making of other men.

Now for Joe that came in the form of Jack Canfield's Chicken Soup For The Soul.

A book loaded with five-minute fables of fortune that force the mind to focus on what the day should and will bring. A switch of standards that he has now also enforced whenever waiting for coffee, standing in a line, or bordering on boredom.

A positive pick-me-up that will protect the mind of any self-made man when he is at his most vulnerable.

THE REVELATION FROM THE LAW

There's a certain freedom that comes from removing your expectations from the weak-willed and the weak-minded, both inside and outside of your circle of influence.

In fact, if any of this rings true there are nine things that I'd urge every man at the helm of a business to stop expecting from others, with immediate effect:

1. **Stop expecting them to live by your standards.**

2. **Stop expecting them to do the right thing.**

3. **Stop expecting them to read your mind.**

4. **Stop expecting them to agree with what you said.**

5. **Stop expecting them to understand.**

6. **Stop expecting them to support you.**

7. **Stop expecting them to treat you like you treat them.**

8. **Stop expecting them to stay the same.**

9. **Stop expecting them to change.**

Doing so finally allows you to focus on what you can control:

YOUR ENVIRONMENT.
YOUR MIND.
YOU.

IRON LAW #4

Never Think Like
An Arsehole

When we were kids, my Grandad used to say, "What are you, boys? Men or mice?"

My brother and I always chose MEN.

Funny thing is, knowing what I know now, I would choose mice – every time.

Why? Because...

Men Think Like Arseholes

This was a phenomenon that the great Werner Erhard explained best in the 1970s.

You see, if you put a hungry mouse in a maze of four tunnels and always put cheese at the end of the fourth one, give it time and the mouse will learn to ALWAYS go down the fourth tunnel to find cheese.

Men will learn to do the same thing too.

If we want cheese, straight to the fourth tunnel we will go.

Over time, it's what we've come to know. It becomes normal. It's where we expect to find the cheese.

Now, let's imagine the cheese moves to another tunnel.

The mouse goes straight to the fourth tunnel – no cheese.

The mouse tries the fourth tunnel again – no cheese.

The mouse comes out of the maze and re-enters the fourth tunnel – still no cheese.

BUT here's the thing, if given enough time, the mouse will eventually switch gears and try all three OTHER tunnels on the hunt for cheese. And here's the kicker – and the difference between mice and men. Men won't switch gears or try other tunnels.

Instead...

Most Men Will Go Down the Same (Wrong) Tunnel Forever

In fact, it's worse. Because not only will we continue to go down that same (wrong) tunnel forever, but we will come to BELIEVE that the fourth tunnel is the right one, regardless of there being cheese or no cheese. We start to believe that because the cheese was there once before, if we just persist and give it time, it must appear there again soon.

This is what Werner Erhard called believing and thinking like an arsehole.

Which is kind of funny, because mice believe in NOTHING. Mice don't give a shit about what they or others believe. Truth is that mice are only interested in one thing – successfully getting cheese.

If you've ever wondered how some people choose to be stuck in the same situation, no matter what – this is why. Instead of choosing to change the tunnel, change the situation or change the way that the game is played, most choose to moan, complain and just carry on believing in the same fourth tunnel, regardless of the output.

I suspect if you're honest with yourself, it's why for a long time now you know you haven't been getting any cheese. You too, my friend, have got too many beliefs in the fourth tunnel. Arsehole beliefs in tunnels that have been systematically installed in you from an early age by parents, teachers and society as a whole.

Is it any wonder that most men on this planet are on their arse by the time they hit 55? Not only that but would it surprise you to find out that most are not only stressed, frustrated and pissed off with their current situation but they no longer trust or believe in themselves or the decisions that they make?

American psychologist Rollo May said it best:

"The opposite of courage in our society is NOT cowardice … it is CONFORMITY."

And there you have it. The reason for so many failures in this game today...

Most Would Rather Conform Than Succeed

Men, conforming, behaving and believing in the same tunnels as all the other arseholes. Brainwashed, battered and bullied into no longer believing in themselves and instead going dazed and confused down the same fourth tunnel just like everyone else – without knowing why or where they are heading.

Funny thing is, most of us learn to walk by the age of one. We learn to read by seven. We learn how to provide for ourselves and our family by the time we hit 30. And yet by the time most hit 55, we're fucked. Why?

Conforming to, and adopting the same arsehole beliefs, in the same arsehole tunnels as the wrong percentage group in society – the 95% who don't, and will never succeed.

I need you to understand that your present situation is a

direct result of the choices that you have made up to this point. Choices to keep conforming to the same arsehole belief systems as the masses.

The Six Fundamental Arsehole Beliefs That Stop Men From Being Free

Arsehole Belief #1: The self-made man can no longer compete. The Tax Cheatin' Corporations are now too powerful to challenge.

One Man Empire Iron Fact #1: At the time of writing this and despite being in the middle of a global pandemic, most would be wise to consider that this could never be further from the truth.

The fact is, there has never been a time where the big corporations have been more vulnerable and open to attack.

The trend over the last decade for corporate restructure after restructure has left the big businesses of value overrun by middle-management and misguided employees. A situation made worse by their culture of "choice by committee", which forces decision making to be slow at best and non-existent at worst.

Meaning that across the board there is a perfect storm for the smart, agile, and ambitious self-made man to transform himself into a One Man Empire with more ease and more speed than ever imaginable.

Arsehole Belief #2: I'm not a "real" businessman and I've got no experience in being one.

One Man Empire Iron Fact #2: The universal fact of life is that no man had experience doing anything until he started doing it.

→ No baby could walk before they started walking.

→ No child could talk before they started talking.

→ No man could provide before they started providing.

Understand that no man has ever run a business until they started running a business. There is no manual, there is no guidebook, there is no blueprint.

The raw fact that you started, and you're still going, puts you amongst a small bracket of men on this planet that have the power in their hands to really control how they choose to provide and protect.

For it is the man that starts doing that learns the quickest.

Arsehole Belief #3: You have to be born lucky.
One Man Empire Iron Fact #3: Bullshit. In my experience the more you work, the luckier you become.

Arsehole Belief #4: Money is the route of all evil.
One Man Empire Iron Fact #4: Money is of vital importance, because without it you're dead in the water. Consider that for men like you and me, money is the best way – the only way – to be rewarded for your work.

Money is the true path to freedom of choice. Now with that freedom comes an almighty power to be able to change people's lives. The pursuit of money, the enjoyment from it and spreading of it should be encouraged at all costs.

Arsehole Belief #5: The self-made man is of low importance and low status.

One Man Empire Iron Fact #5: The man at the helm of his own business is arguably the most important member of modern society as we know it. For it's the self-made man and his natural drive to put others before himself that keeps the wheels of commerce turning.

For the self-made man is an individual that must bring certainty to chaos, calm to confusion and confidence to clutter.

He must be able to build relationships, innovate, organise, plan, negotiate, sell and most of all live and die by his own sword, for like many spartan warriors it's his decisions that determine if he comes back with his shield, or on it.

It's this type of man that's the backbone of every modern society and every great nation of value. Without the jobs he provides, the taxes he pays, and the self that he sacrifices, society would grind to a halt.

Arsehole Belief #6: Selling is bad and should be avoided at all costs.

One Man Empire Iron Fact #6: In this game today, understand that nothing happens until a sale is made.

Those who deem selling as evil, do not understand:

➡ **Selling is what puts food on the table.**

➡ **Selling is what puts roofs over heads.**

➔ Selling is what keeps the wolves from the door.

In fact, I'd go as far as to say that it's a moral obligation of every self-made man to study the art and science of how to sell himself, sell his wares and sell his vision for the future.

For it is only in selling that change can be made.

THE REVELATION FROM THE LAW

STOP Conforming

Instead, I urge you to step up and believe in the man YOU were born to be. And arm that man to the nines. That means you, my friend, making a conscious choice to choose new tunnels and...

➔ Start accepting yourself as YOU.

➔ Start believing and trusting in YOU.

➔ Start feeling free to express who You are and what YOU want to be.

➔ Start knowing YOUR strengths and YOUR weaknesses.

➔ And start being honest about the choices YOU make and the way YOU think.

Start Choosing New Tunnels

You see there is power in making choices. There is power in understanding how you and I have been contributing to our current situation. And there is power in finally knowing that you, and only you, can choose to make the change.

But first, in order to harness that power, you need to be able to see the wood through the trees and spot your current tunnel of choice – your fourth tunnel.

IRON LAW #5

Anger Always
Stops Action

"FUCK YOU – I'm doing this for us."

It's 7.14 a.m., and I'm already halfway through my default defence against the persecution at home, and against the business – not how I expected to start this particular Saturday morning.

Especially because all I wanted to do was sleep. It had been another week of 16-hour days, trying to get things over the line and off my list.

This time the catalyst for being backed into a corner and called out on my shit, was the fact that I was on my phone (again) in bed.

In my defence, I was dealing with a client. But on reflection, two weeks previously I'd promised not to work at weekends. Barney was just three weeks away from being born and I'd made a bold and empty declaration that "things were going to change".

I can see it now. Truth is, the older I've got the angrier and more irritable I've become. Not just at home but over stupid shit elsewhere too – normally things I couldn't control or had no influence over whatsoever.

Tiny little things that get my blood racing from 0 to 100 mile per hour in about three seconds flat. A notion that would set the day off on the wrong foot and leave things going from bad to worse. You see...

Rage Festers, Infects and Rots the Mind of Man

This is something that I've come to understand to be somewhat out of my control, and is all down to the way that most men are hard-wired from the inside out.

Case in point: Here is the default source code that most men operate when pissed off, their back's up against the wall or the shit hits the fan:

1. Have a triggered reaction that you've been wronged.

2. Tell yourself a story about what's happened.

3. Find evidence to support that story.

4. Ignore all evidence that says otherwise.

5. When people try to help, get more frustrated and pissed off because they don't understand.

A pattern of thought that's dictated by trigger then response. Or in other words, a straight-line process that in the heat of the moment causes a reaction of flash fire and fury.

Or worse, you get to a place where that rage is not released and is allowed to fester. A place where you choose to keep things pent-up, locked-up and bottled-up until breaking point – and then it's time to unleash fire and fury on whoever gets caught in the crossfire.

And here's the problem for men like you and I, that choose to operate with the same source code as the mass mediocre majority:

➜ Anger always starts overwhelm.

➜ Anger always starts persecution.

➜ Anger always starts panic.

A place which all but forces a downward spiral and rapid descent into no man's land. Made worse of course because right now there have never been so many triggers and stressors for modern man.

There Are Six Reasons for Rage in the Self-made Man:

1. Customers who don't pay on time, make dickhead demands, have no respect and want everything doing right now and on their schedule.

THE "FORBIDDEN" SECRETS OF A ONE MAN EMPIRE

2. **Employees** who don't do as they are told, can't follow instructions, are lazy, do the bare minimum, have no drive and are constantly making demands of you, your time and your energy.

3. **The Government** who seems to be expecting the self-made man to do more and more, for less and less.

4. **Competitors** who drop their pants on price, do a shit job, lie in their marketing and try to steal your customers from under your nose.

5. **Society** that chastises success, thrives on political correctness and operates a strict backlash against most things male.

6. **Family** for enforcing guilt.

When it's laid out like that, in the cold, hard light of day, is it any wonder that most men in this game are left increasingly strained and mentally fucked?

There Is Power and Control in Unleashing the Rage

"Between stimulus and response there is a space. In that space is our power to choose our response."
– Viktor Frankl

When it comes to the stressors that plague men in this game today, it is imperative that we understand these triggers, the specifics that grind gears and get backs up. So that we can spot the warning signs before the rage punches us square in the mouth.

The game then becomes hijacking the default source code of mediocrity to create space and release any rage before responding.

Because it's in that space – and with the rage already released – that power is created, and control is seized with full force.

Unleashing the rage with fire and fury and in a controlled environment creates that space, and that space allows men to take the upper hand mentally; control thought patterns, control conscious thinking and most importantly control how we CHOOSE to respond.

Meaning now more than ever your source code for responding to stressors and triggers must become:

1. **Have a triggered reaction that you've been wronged.**

2. **Create space to unleash any rage with fire and fury (without being an arsehole).**

3. **Choose a considered response.**

Prime example below – my private journal entry from November 14th, 2020:

"You fucking moron. That is the stupidest thing I've ever heard. Waiting for the New Year is going to BURY YOU. You've just told me your competitors are coming and your customers are leaving. Your family is depending on you NOW – NOT THEN. Fuck, I can't believe you are even entertaining this idea. If I see you bitching and moaning online that everything's gone to rat shit, it will be your own fucking fault. How dare you waste my time on the phone by using this as an excuse to be a lazy piece of shit. ARRRRRRRGH. IDIOT. How do these people manage to get up and survive in the real world? Fuck me!!!!"

It was something I immediately unleashed and screamed onto the page after an interview with a potential candidate for The One Man Empire Fellowship. Needless to say, he didn't cut the mustard and won't be coming to join us around the table.

Point is, in that moment I knew this arsehole had the possibility to trigger an emotional response. So space was created where that emotion could be unleashed at full force, unfiltered and without repercussion.

Lesson being, men like you and I can't afford to let anything stew.

Anger and resentment are the curse of the self-made man. Always, always, ALWAYS let it out with hellfire and fury on paper and without the filter, before any response.

THE REVELATION FROM THE LAW

The man who has total control is always the man who understands his triggers, and creates space in order to respond with poise and consideration.

Remember, anger always stops a man dead in his tracks. It is the Achilles heel and the stake in the heart for too many men in this game today.

Whenever pissed off, frustrated or needing to scream bloody murder at someone, it's your moral obligation to immediately write down – unfiltered – exactly what you NEED to unleash to their face, but can't because that would make you an arsehole.

The pure action of putting pen to paper always:

→ Unleashes the fire and fury.

→ Empowers you, not them.

→ And puts you back in control.

Building Unshakeable Mental Muscle with The Iron Laws of Man

How One Man Empire and Accountant, Adam Warner Is Back in the Saddle and Going Full Bore, Even After Hitting Rock Bottom (Twice)...

When Adam took the bold move to separate from his wife, he was at rock bottom and almost at breaking point. All he had and hoped he needed was his mental grit and determination as a self-made man to see him through, and back on top.

It Can Happen to Any Man

In 2017, he relapsed for the second time in two months, falling face first and back into No Man's Land – a situation triggered by Adam's belief that he could work his way out of his problems.

"I was always told that as a 'successful' business owner, I should be grateful for what I have… That I was 'lucky' to have what they deemed as 'flexibility'," commented Adam. "Thing is, I was fucked. Struggling mentally and physically with the fatigue and persecution that doing all of this alone entails."

A reality and a situation that led Adam to setting some big hairy goals for the next 12 months, in one last-ditch attempt to try and turn it all around. "I've never felt so overwhelmed," reflected Adam as he recalled waking up every morning feeling like a failure. One thing after another seemingly stopping every single goal dead in its tracks.

"It was like having your face constantly rubbed in all the shit, that for one reason or another, you hadn't achieved or hadn't accomplished."

Not one to back down from a challenge, Adam started looking for ideas and inspiration and that's when he came across the Iron Laws of Man and raised daily standards.

Daily Non-Negotiables

"It just made much sense. So right there and on the spot, my goals got burnt to the ground and I started operating by a new code of conduct in all areas of my life."

Setting in stone daily standards like:

- A non-negotiable 45 minutes of weights in the morning.
- A non-negotiable locking the phone away in the evening.
- And a non-negotiable hard hour drumming up new work every morning.

"The impact was almost immediate," remarked Adam as he reflected on his first week operating in this new way. "Mentally I was more free and physically I had never felt in such control. The funny thing was after about three weeks, those daily standards become second nature – meaning I didn't even need to think about it, they just happened."

"My biggest trouble was that I kept getting dragged back to the bottom of the barrel whenever around friends – especially old ones," he commented.

"At the time, I needed other men around me for mental support. But when I started dissecting my friendship circle at the time, I noticed that Mike was unemployed, James was divorced and Pete was living with his parents – at 42! A coincidence that I was where I was? Probably not!"

Quickly and with full force, Adam tells of the time, he cut all ties and started choosing new tunnels. "I started questioning everything, and my new rule of thumb became: if people are doing one thing, I'm pretty sure the safest bet is to do the exact opposite."

A mantra for money that has served him well since. Today, Adam talks about his new-found unshakeable CONFIDENCE, and the knock-on effect it seems to have had when it comes to loyalty and respect from others – both customers and those outside of work too.

"This gives me real excitement for the future," Adam says. "I'm more confident and more at peace than ever and it's paying dividends."

To read more about Adam see:
http://warneraccountants.co.uk/

PART 2

THE UNIVERSAL IRON LAWS OF
MONEY

"Money Can Buy Many Things. Even Power. The Road To Our Future Begins Here, My Friend."

- Vladimir Makarov

IRON LAW #6

Ruthlessly Disregard Bad Money

This is an email received by Karl Lehmann – One Man Empire and the individual at the helm of a Financial Advisory practice in South Devon – at 7.18 p.m. on August 16th, 2019:

Karl, you might be right.

But I've tried five or six other financial advisors before, and after a couple of months, I've found they've not delivered what I wanted. So why should I choose you? Anyone including me can now go online and do it myself.

Why should I believe this will do what I want, and trust that you can do it for me?

If you can let me know SPECIFICALLY what

you can do for me, I might be interested!

Keep up the great work!

Hmm… Do you see what I see?

I mean, you can smell it a mile off – the RED FLAG, that says this person is a massive pain in the arse and wants the moon on a stick. With the kicker being, he's tried "five or six things" before.

I mean fuck, if history has taught me anything it's that after the third divorce it's YOU, not them. And in my experience, that's never more true than when a lead or a prospect reaches out who's already "tried everything else".

You know the kind of customer I'm talking about, the ones whose CV reads like this:

"I am a special snowflake. My situation is nothing like you've dealt with before. I'm more important than everything else you've got going on, including your wife and kids. In fact, nothing is my fault and if you don't do what I demand then I will throw my toys out of the pram."

Rightly, Karl told this particular arsehole where to go jump.

But if you've ever experienced any significant highs or lows when running a business then you know the drill. When the money dips, your back's against the wall, and the shit's about to hit the fan, you don't see the red flags or the warning signs – you just take the money.

Blinded by a Natural Desperation to Provide Any Money at All Costs

All hands on deck as you try to "just sell" anything to anyone. Even to miserable men like this, who lack backbone and have a God complex. As a man, your natural instinct to provide takes hold and with it so does an acceptance and willingness to make any money, from anyone, for anything – regardless of the repercussions.

Backed up by the arsehole belief system that all money is created equal – when it's not.

I've been there, especially after my son was born. I was desperate to give him more than I had growing up, yet the money wasn't there. I was chasing project after project on the desperate hunt for 'more', whatever the cost and whatever the consequence.

And herein lies the problem.

Desperation Only Provides Bad Money

Case in point: Have you ever been in a situation when you REALLY needed to make a sale?

It's the hardest time to get money over the line. People can smell desperation a mile off. It's why desperation repels good money and always attracts bad.

And always why when operating in a state of desperation to provide more money, it's so easy to lose control:

→ Taking on bad clients.

→ Taking on bad projects.

➜ Taking on bad debts.

Here's the kicker – bad money makes you think you are providing more, but the fact of the matter is:

There Is No Profit in Bad Money

Here's why:

➜ Bad money wants you available 24/7.

➜ Bad money wants more than what's agreed.

➜ Bad money questions the price (more than once).

➜ Bad money has unrealistic expectations.

➜ Bad money doesn't know what it wants.

➜ Bad money won't commit to anything.

➜ Bad money wants ideas for free.

➜ Bad money is never quite satisfied.

➜ Bad money is late and never paid on time.

➜ Bad money moves the goalposts.

→ Bad money pushes your personal boundaries.

If you've ever felt overworked and underpaid, despite the business turning over more money, this is the reason why. Bad money is only working for revenue whereas good money is always working for profit.

You must get clear on the difference between the two, and understand that one provides hard work, while the other provides money in your back-pocket (aka freedom).

Understand That Good Money Loves Clarity

Funny thing is, I suspect that – if you're like the other men that have taken this path before – then money is important, but it's not the be-all and end-all. It's why what constitutes good money is different for every man that plays this game. And why you need to get crystal-clear clarity on what good money looks like for you.

Let me explain. Last year, I turned down a six-figure project with a "celebrity" (there's a watertight NDA in place so legally I cannot disclose names).

After a lot of negotiation back and forth, an online meeting was set for Thursday at 3.25 p.m. to discuss the possibilities of a project. Now here's the kicker, when Thursday rolled round, this guy was late. Very late. In fact, 17 minutes and 26 seconds late AND with zero communication to explain why.

Needless to say, I decided to end the relationship there and then and without any further conversations.

Now, most would think turning down this kind of money

over timekeeping is lunacy of the highest order, but that would be arsehole thinking.

See, I hate lateness. It shows lack of care. It shows a lack of organisation. And ultimately it shows no respect. Truth be told, it only demonstrates that they value their time more than they value yours. And let's be clear, if this is the way the first meeting goes, you can only imagine how the rest of the project is going to go – south, quickly.

Demonstration off the bat that this project was going to be the wrong kind of money, BAD MONEY.

It's why you must get crystal-clear clarity on what good and bad money is for you, your business and your situation.

Without it, the strategic decision of "should I do this" is an impossible one to make.

Meaning your next step moving forward is to...

Decide What You Won't Do for Money

Or in other words, the creation of a BIG list of NOs, that will become your Rules of Engagement.

The measuring stick on how you will start making the right decisions around the money that comes into your business, to ensure you only choose projects, customers and contracts that are made up of GOOD money.

A code of conduct that gets included in emails, contracts and even on the wall so that everyone in the business is crystal clear and on the same page:

Case in point: Andy Rao and Joel Stone, men at the helm of Codebreak, a fast-paced marketing and design agency. Pissed off and frustrated with being overworked and underpaid, they installed the following Rules Of Engagement to take back control of the money inside their business:

1. **Rule #1** – Lateness will not be tolerated, so be on time for all calls and all meetings.

2. **Rule #2** – All meetings and phone calls must be planned in advance.

3. **Rule #3** – No email contact outside of Monday-Friday, 9 a.m.-5 p.m.

4. **Rule #4** – Overdue payments will result in things being immediately turned off.

5. **Rule #5** – No work will be done without a brief.

Now Here's What That Means in Reality:

There was finally a clear line drawn in the sand that differentiated what was good money and what was bad. Now here's what that means in reality for Andy and Joel and their business: the low-end, low-paid, high-effort jobs are stopped before they even get off the ground.

Or in other words, they now get paid what they deserve, on projects that they deem to be a good fit for them, their business and their future.

THE REVELATION FROM THE LAW

The self-made man of value understands that this game is OURS to play, which means YOU get to choose the rules. YOU get to choose who you take money from, and YOU get to choose how you take it and on what terms.

So if you smell a rat, run a mile. Or even better, send them to a competitor and let them deal with the ball ache.

Control Only Comes From Attracting Good Money

It will always come to those who ruthlessly choose to enforce it. This is what happens when those around you see that you are taking control of the cash conundrum in your business:

→ Respect increases as you start demonstrating you are the one in control, not them.

→ Loyalty increases as you start attracting customers that value you and what you do.

➔ Cash increases as you finally start seeing profit coming into the business.

IRON LAW #7

No Dickheads Allowed

Shit. It's Saturday morning, and I've got a BIG customer on the phone – again.

"You and me are going to have problems..."

That was how he started his verbal onslaught of demands. And in a flash, I'm an insecure 13-year-old boy again. Now, high school is supposed to mould you as a man. But for me, I never felt like I really fitted in.

I had friends, lots of them, but school was a battle. A chubby teenager, trying to fit into the new order of man by constantly submitting to peers, backed by a childhood instinct to want to please others.

A state of mind that as we grow older leads to being stuck somewhere between a "puppet on a string" and a "pushover".

Bending over backwards for the demands of others – especially customers.

The Achilles heel, and the chink in the armour when it comes to men like you and I sacrificing control. Made worse by the old adage and deep-rooted arsehole belief that "the customer is always right" – no matter what.

Customers Are Where the Problems Start for Most

Which brings me back to that Saturday morning and this dickhead customer. You see, three days earlier – and against my better judgement – I agreed to help. And let's be clear this help was outside of our contract, outside of our agreement and outside of our time allocated.

In other words, I was helping an existing customer, for free. Because he'd asked, and because I was being nice. This phone call was a direct result of him not being happy with the "FREE" help my business had provided.

My diagnosis?

If You Give Them an Inch, They Will Take a Mile

Which is why, in my opinion, some customers are dumb, stupid and should be avoided at all costs!

Chances are if you've ever seen a customer's name flash up on email, on the phone, or in a message and thought, "fuck… them again," then I suspect you already know first-hand exactly what I'm talking about.

Which begs the question, why do we always place the customer as the King Of The Hill?

Because here's the problem when you do.

It Puts Them in Control

And it empowers them, NOT you. And here's what most don't realise about the practical implications of that power transfer:

→   You lose your respect.

→   You lose your loyalty.

→   You lose your peace of mind.

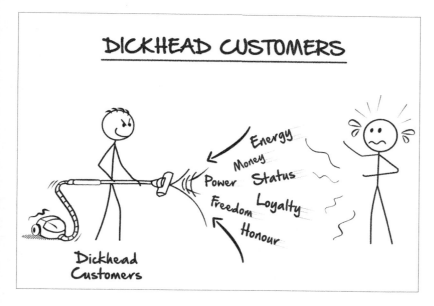

The funny thing is, this shift is subtle yet the consequences for you and your control can be catastrophic. Which is why when it comes to customers you want to look out for any that are:

→   Demanding you give free help.

➜ Demanding you pick up the phone when it rings.

➜ Demanding you reply to an email as soon as it pings.

➜ Demanding you do anything and everything for them, at the drop of a hat, even out-of-hours and at the weekend.

Because truth be told, in the cold, hard light of day...

If Not Controlled, Good Money Can – and Will – Always Turn Bad

The all-too-familiar situation of a cash cow becoming a poisoned chalice. Sometimes it's a week, sometimes it's a month, sometimes it's a year or even more, but it's never a matter of IF it's ALWAYS a matter of WHEN.

And when that tipping point is reached, you must take that customer out to the field and deliver a swift bullet to the head. No matter how long they've been with your business and no matter how much money they've passed your way.

Tenure and Monetary Value Is No Excuse for Being a Dick

The point you need to understand is that just because they are an existing customer, you don't have to keep taking their money.

In fact, unless you are contractually obliged, I'll have you consider:

➜   You don't have to answer their calls.

➜   You don't have to reply to their emails.

➜   You don't have to obey their demands.

Because you, my friend, have the power to choose to totally ignore their noise.

Stopping the ensuing stress, fatigue and panic that they bring – dead in its tracks. Meaning you can choose to continue enjoying your evenings, your weekends and your day-to-day life by refusing to respond when the bell rings. Or better still:

You Must Sack All Toxic and Dickhead Customers

I remember being sat across the table from the great Dan Kennedy who muttered these fateful words to the room:

"A sacked toxic customer will always be quickly replaced by someone better..."

A very real phenomenon I have witnessed and experienced over and over and over again. It's why every quarter I urge you to run a PURGE to eradicate any and all blood-sucking leeches from your business.

The Purge
verb

A process for customer control, where the poor, the time-intensive, and annoying are weeded out for the benefit of the high-paying, fun to work with, and profitable... so you no longer have to sacrifice time (or money) to keep dickhead customers happy or onboard.

In other words, it's a process to regularly sack customers that have gone bad. Because life is too short. Especially when there are other people that should be allowed to demand more of your time than is currently on offer.

Now, here's a good rule of thumb to determine which customers should go and which customers should stay.

Start asking yourself this question: How do you feel when you see their name pop up on your phone?

If the answer is: "Oh shit, it's them – again!"

Then, my friend, it's time to sack them and eradicate them from your business immediately.

Sacking Customers Will Actually Make You Money

Take Steve Timmis, the man at the helm of an accounting practice. Now Steve was on a slippery slope. The occasional late night at the office had fast become a daily ritual of not setting foot back in the house much before 8 p.m., 9 p.m., and more often than not 11 p.m. in the evening – after a 6 a.m. start.

Unfortunately, his home life wasn't the only thing that was suffering at the hands of this "successful" growth. Over the last six months Steve had begun noticing that not only was he personally hitting Overstretch, but members of his eleven-strong team were too.

Leaving a toxic atmosphere of back-biting and undermining starting to take control inside of the office. It was at that moment that Steve started running the numbers. Interestingly he found that 20% of his clients were requiring 80% of his time. Made worse by the fact that it was this same 20% that were paying the least AND demanding the most.

Which Just Goes to Show the Dickhead Demands Must Stop

It's why Steve decided that the 20% must go, and be SACKED in one giant client cull. A BIG gamble, especially when you consider that this immediately wiped a huge chunk off the bottom line of his business, at a time when he had 11 people expecting a paycheque at the end of the month.

The upshot being that Steve and his business could finally

focus on serving his higher-paying customers that were more deserving of the time, the energy and the attention. Something in turn that allowed them to start creating more opportunities, to sell more services, to more existing clients.

Empowering Steve to focus on starting to attract more of the RIGHT kind of customers to fill the void.

The funny thing was, it only took Steve and his team 31 days to replace the customers that had been sacked.

The good news about this is that all of the new clients were hand-picked and scored against Steve's NEW Rules Of Engagement – meaning they were more profitable and less work. Twelve months on and Steve has doubled his business, and done so without sacrificing control at home or work to any dickhead customers.

THE REVELATION FROM THE LAW

The self-made man understands that there is REAL POWER in choosing with whom you do business.

The good news is that when you do:

➔ **You stop panicking when the phone rings.**

➔ **You stop being held to ransom to dickhead demands.**

➔ **You stop the relentless pressure of being bent over a barrel in the evenings and at the weekends, and you can finally start taking back control.**

I have sacked no fewer than 10 customers over the last five years and have not regretted a single one. Some I personally liked. Some I still personally call friends. BUT all demanded that I sacrificed my control, for them. So they had to go. In every instance:

→ **It increases respect.**

→ **It increases loyalty.**

→ **It increases freedom.**

IRON LAW #8

Despise Earning Money

If life has taught me anything as a man in today's game, it's seven deadly sins or what I call "Never, Evers". Seven hard lines in the sand, that in no way, shape or form, should ever be violated in the new emerging order of man:

1. Never ever wear thongs or speedos.

2. Never ever attempt to wear leather trousers.

3. Never ever pretend to be someone else.

4. Never ever change your dreams, goals and ambitions for others.

5. Never ever get in touch with your feminine side.

6.   Never ever tell your wife she's overeating.

7.   Never ever earn money.

Truth is I have made the first six mistakes but never the seventh. That one, a long time ago, I set in stone, and to this day guard with an iron first.

It comes down to this:

Earnt Money Is Always Bad Money

Let me explain. You see Earnt Money, is a train of thought that forces the man at the helm of the business (even with employees) to operate on the tools and on the clock that is:

➔   Accountants doing the accounting.

➔   Bakers doing the baking.

➔   Builders doing the building.

➔   Hairdressers doing the cutting.

➔   Lawyers doing the lawyering.

Meaning for the man at the top, the lion's share of his time is spent doing what the business does. A conscious choice to continue to operate like an employee by trading time for money – and earning it.

A catalyst that means everything else inside of the business slowly grinds to a halt, because those that subscribe to "earning" are always focused on:

→ Earning enough money to pay the bills.

→ Earning enough money to pay others.

→ Earning enough money to SURVIVE.

Backed-up with an arsehole belief that no one else can do anything as well as they can.

Resulting in a never-ending daily battle of grunt work, firefights and capped income. Truth is, as an earner, most won't get paid much more than an employee who completes the same task.

Meaning that when the rubber hits the road, the overwhelming majority of those operating at the helm of a business, while thinking within the realms of earning money, are nothing more than employees suffering from delusions of grandeur.

You see...

Earning Money Is Where the Trouble Starts for Most

As you will start to discover in **Part 3 The Universal Laws Of Freedom**, in most situations the physical "doing" can, and must, be purchased, out-sourced and even automated at all costs.

Which begs the question as of right now, and in this instance...

Are You Spending Too Much Time Earning Money to Make a Real Living?

The fact of the matter is, most have no clue until they start to run the numbers and see what their time is really worth.

So when all's said and done, let's start exploring your current hourly rate and what it should be worth:

$$\text{Current Hourly Rate} = \frac{\$ \underline{\quad} \text{ earned a week}}{\underline{\quad} \text{ hours worked a week}}$$

So let's say for example you work a 50 hour week and take home $2000, you are currently valuing your time at the helm of your business at $40 / hour.

Now let's flip that on its head and look at what that time needs to be worth for you to hit your income goal.

For the sake of argument today let's assume you'd consider taking home $250,000 / year (approx. $4,800 / week) to be a success, and that you'd like to do that by spending 30 hours a week operating in your business.

$$\text{Target Hourly Rate} = \frac{\text{Target } \$ \underline{\quad} \text{ earned a week}}{\text{Target } \underline{\quad} \text{ hours worked a week}}$$

Making your target hourly rate $160 / hour.

Yes, that's right. And in other words, at a current rate of $40

/ hour right now, you are off the mark by a mind-blowing $120 / hour.

It's why for any self-made man, understanding his worth is so important.

1. It shines a light on why, despite working more, you might at best be standing still or worse going backwards.

2. It becomes a measuring stick for where your time should be spent and where you must leverage others to step in and step up.

Meaning...

You Must Let Others Earn Money for You, So You Can Print It

Now, if you're sat there thinking:

FUCK – Charlie how the hell do I achieve that rate, every hour, of every day?

Consider that based on **Iron Law #1: Relentlessly Resist Being Overstretched, to Prevent Being Royally Fucked**, the answer will not be found in doing more work.

The fact of the matter is that this new economy dictates the answer can only be found in building a scalable empire that provides maximum leverage.

And by leverage, I mean TIME – or what we call here the ability to print money.

Think of McDonald's.

When Ray Crock bought McDonald's from the McDonald brothers, they had one outlet. Ray's One Man Empire has now served over 1 billion burgers worldwide. And in the cold, hard light of day Ray has not flipped a single one. Instead he learned to LEVERAGE his time elsewhere in the business, so he could start printing more money per hour than he could ever earn.

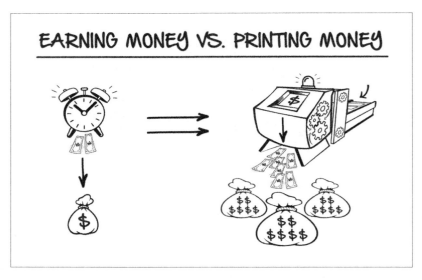

EARNING MONEY VS. PRINTING MONEY

See, the highest payoff activity for the self-made man will always be those strategic actions that allow you to start printing money. And in my experience the only action that consistently prints money, time and time again, is:

MARKETING.

An Efficient Marketing System Is the Only Way to *Legally* Print Money

Because effective marketing should reliably print at least

one additional dollar for every dollar invested. Making it your duty from today and moving forward to down tools and start thinking about:

→ The creation of marketing systems.

→ The creation of marketing campaigns.

→ The creation of marketing offers.

The very same kind of marketing strategies and tactics that are laid bare in my bestselling book The Orgasm Effect - The Business Owners Guide to Get Customers Screaming...Yes, Yes, YES! Available in bookstores or from online booksellers. Additional information at www.charliehutton.co.uk/books.

Suggesting that as this new economy takes its grip, your ultimate success is not dependent on working more to earn more, but instead IS dependent on you being able to leverage your business to effortlessly print money.

That is the printing of money by focusing your time, energy and effort on magnetically attracting good quality, high-paying customers that keep spending money.

See printing money, by its nature, dictates that a man understands down to his core, his biggest opportunity to truly provide and protect is in making the fundamental shift from "on the tools" to "in the business".

Or in other words, unlocking the power transfer that comes from being the MARKETER, not the doer.

THE REVELATION FROM THE LAW

The self-made man understands that there is a sense of power in being able to CONTROL the flow of customers coming through the door. A certainty that comes from being truly self-sufficient. A sense of possibility and realisation, that YES they are in control of how the business truly provides. And no, I'm not just talking about providing and printing money.

Sure the new cars are nice, and the three or four holidays a year are a good side effect of what all of that brings. But I'm talking about providing something else too:

→   Providing a freedom of choice.

→   Providing a freedom of stability.

→   And providing the freedom of time.

Something that most of us took this leap of faith for in the first place, and something that will always be out of reach and beyond grasp, while subscribing to "earning" over "printing".

IRON LAW #9

Isolation Is Deadly: Keep An Iron Council

A wise man once said, there are two types of people in this world – the mediocre majority and us.

If history has taught me anything, it's that being our kind of "unemployable" is a line drawn in the sand. A rare genetic mutation that often rears its head at a young age. I was 15 when I first discovered that I could pay my own way, selling homemade fake IDs in the playground at school.

Even back then, I knew I wasn't one of them. Deep down most feel it, and it's only a matter of time before it becomes clear as day.

You and I Are the Elephants in the Room

Friends, foes and family members tiptoeing around the topic of what we do and why we do it. A dripping tap of doom, gloom and doubt. Every single word, sentence and snipe, laced with misplaced opinions and hidden agendas. A sobering, self-imposed state of suffering and silence.

Which begs the question: Why are those who are closest to us the ones to hold us back the most?

Why are those we love the ones who tell us that this game, this business and this life is too much of a risk? That for the sake of the family we should slow down and play it safe?

The funny thing is, if you ask them to their face, most will say that they want us to be our best. But it seems at every turn they try to stop us from taking the steps most needed to keep pushing forward.

Truth is, it's because...

They Don't Think Like We Think

You see, as physiologists tell us, the human brain is hard-wired for survival. In other words, our brain's number one priority is to keep us safe and away from harm.

Now the important thing about that is that most people don't think like we think. Which means most people don't calculate risk like we calculate risk. It's why the mass mediocre majority see change as something that should be feared and as a vehicle that brings no good.

A state of mind that forces them to believe that in order to stay safe, you must stay the same.

It's why they want you to keep doing what's familiar to them. Because to them, that's what support is, that's what being there is and that's what love is.

Case in point: My old man. He worked for the same

company, man and boy – from 16 until 60. Now, there's nothing wrong with a job for life, but when in my late twenties I moved back to the UK to start my own business his words of advice were these:

"You should get a job."

Here's the thing, my dad is the most supportive man you can imagine. Without him I would not be where I am today or have had the opportunities to travel the world playing hockey. Yet in that moment his instincts as a parent meant he wanted to keep me SAFE.

Now because a job is familiar to him, in his mind it meant that in order to keep me safe, I should choose employee over entrepreneur. Or in other words, I should choose earning money, not printing it.

Yes, he loves me. Yes, he thinks he's offering the right advice. BUT yes, he has a built-in, limiting bias.

It's Why Loved Ones Stop the Movement of Money Dead in Its Tracks

You see, what most don't realise is that this kind of counsel forces us all to be shackled by a limited perspective around money – spending 24 hours a day, seven days a week, locked inside of our own bubble.

Sure some come up for air every once in a while, but when push comes to shove, the opinions that we hear the most are limited to those around us who want to keep us safe.

It's little wonder EVERY successful man that has ever

walked this planet, has sought outside counsel from other like-minded men. These men (athletes, CEOs of Fortune 500 companies, presidents and world leaders) already understand that their limited experience is only a small piece of the puzzle, and that they need outside perspective from others outside of their own chambers.

It's why the Romans invented the Senate and why Napoleon Hill introduced the concept of a mastermind group. To provide an island of sanity and outside perspective to the man who is king of his own kingdom. A carefully assembled council designed to challenge perspective, challenge ideas and challenge long-standing arsehole thinking, no matter how difficult it is to hear.

It's Time to Choose Outside Counsel and Choose That Counsel Wisely

Consider that to successfully navigate this journey, the goal must be to assemble a group of other ambitious men around you, that have zero agendas.

→ Other self-made men who are committed to doing something specific.

→ Other self-made men who have major goals and high standards.

→ Other self-made men who know exactly what they want and are determined to get it.

→ Other self-made men who if asked direct

questions will give you direct answers.

→ Other self-made men who will be found at the front of any pack.

→ Other self-made men who never offer excuses or blame others for mistakes.

→ Other self-made men who if they do not know the answer will say so frankly and honestly.

That is, other like-minded men from other walks of life, that will hold you accountable to a higher standard than you will hold yourself. That will force you to take outside counsel and outside perspective.

You see, ruthlessly pushing forward is impossible without the cooperation and positive input of other smart, ambitious men standing at your side. Men who hold you accountable to every action you promise and every oath that you swear.

Because Money Will Only Freely Flow When Ruthlessly Held to Account

You see, it's one thing to say shit's going to happen. It's another thing to tell your wife that shit is going to change. BUT it's quite another to stand up and be counted by a council of other self-made men.

Other smart, ambitious individuals to whom you have sworn an oath. A promise of action that in the cold, hard light of day shit will get done. A promise that shit will get deployed. A promise that from this point forward you will stand and deliver.

This, my friend, is the kind of hard-core accountability that turns excuses into execution and movement into money.

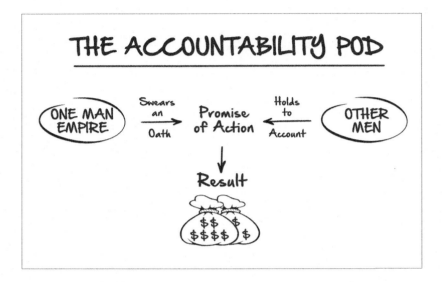

THE REVELATION FROM THE LAW

The smart, ambitious self-made man understands that there is POWER in controlling his council and from whom he takes perspective.

You see this, my friend, is how you gather outside intelligence, outside information and outside ideas to tune and tweak your thoughts, your business and your situation, without any hidden agenda.

This right here is how the most successful men that walk this planet take control of their situation and start making better decisions faster, and start solving complex problems quicker.

Truth is, this is exactly why I always lift weights with a spotter. And not just any old, run-of-the-mill gym rat but a monster of a man that will push me beyond my limits and then keep adding on weight.

Because there's a funny thing that happens when you load up a bar with six 20s and have someone smouldering, sweating and screaming in your face:

"LIFT, LIFT, LIFT."

... the fucking bar moves!

Doubling Turnover and Increasing Profit By 130%

Two Men Have The Iron Laws of Money Challenge Every Aspect of What They Thought Was Possible as Self-Made Men.

Neil and Ian confessed they had tried a lot of "new" things before unlocking the power harnessed by the Iron Laws of Money. "Because we operate a business of 27 people, at first I wasn't 100% sure this was for us," remembered Ian as him and Neil looked back on the start of their journey three short years ago. "Having seen the money we've produced since then, operating like a One Man Empire could not have been a better fit."

Beyond The Plateau

Just five years after starting Acorn Analytical Services, the pair had seen their vision grow beyond what they could have imagined. "We wanted to take on the world, and that meant we grew fast. Both in terms of revenue and bodies in the business," recalled Ian.

Trouble was, after a point they ground to a standstill. The all too familiar story of fast growth followed by paralysing plateau. "We were just getting pulled from pillar to post," remarked Ian. "YES we'd built a successful business, but fuck, were we having to earn our money."

"Overstretch wasn't even the half of it," said Neil as they reflected on what they had really built.

Dickhead Customers

The Achilles heel and fly in the ointment for the pair and their operation was one customer.

The same customer that up until that point had helped their growth by supplying a steady stream of work, projects and income. A relationship that was good in the beginning but had fast become a thorn in their side as the customer started digging in their heels and throwing their toys out of the pram.

Now, for Neil and Ian this was a situation that reached boiling point as Ian's role evolved from business developer to babysitter. "In all honesty I came to the realisation that I was their bitch," laughed Ian as he looked back on the situation.

"The worst part was we'd started this business for more freedom, yet here I was, in the evenings and weekends chained to my phone, my email and my direct dial."

The straw that broke the camel's back was the fallout from Ian being unavailable for a four-hour period while he celebrated an anniversary with his wife Sian. "I had 16 missed calls, 4 text messages and 6 emails all demanding that I drop everything and pick up the phone," exclaimed Ian.
It was at this moment that Ian realised this good customer had turned bad. The next morning they sat down and sacked that customer from the business – choosing to veto all projects, proposals and profits that they presented or pushed their way.

In that instance, the duo doubled down and put together strict rules of engagement that ensured they were never backed into a corner again. "It's funny," said Ian, "there's a real sense of power that comes from dictating terms to customers rather than it being the other way around."

Finally Printing Money

"With that monkey off our backs we choose to put all our focus into marketing," said Neil. "Truth is we'd done a little bit before but had never managed to turn it into a real machine that prints money."
With a little bit of guidance from their Iron Council and accountability pod, within a few short months they turned the Asbestos industry on its head. "All of a sudden we'd walk into a room full of strangers and people knew who we were. We were overnight industry celebrities," exclaimed Ian.

The direct result of their efforts to launch and put into place:

- A book on Amazon.
- A podcast on iTunes.
- And a documentary online.

A marketing machine that most multinational companies wouldn't even believe was doable.

"If you'd asked us 18 months ago if it was possible to do any of those things, I'd have said bullshit. Yet here we are. Proof in the pudding that there's something about sitting across the table and seeing other men taking action. It holds you to account and forces you to consider how much untapped potential you really have," said Ian.

Does This Work?

Eight months on from that crucial client cull and the business is stronger than ever.

"This year turnover has jumped from $1.5m to $2.7m, and pre-tax profit is up 130%. Funny thing is I've never felt more in control," Neil laughed as he and Ian reminisced.

Ian finished with, "For me the real freedom has come from finally having a money-making machine. There is something about knowing that while I'm hunting, fishing or on the bike, the business is literally printing money thanks to the marketing machine we have put in place."

To read more about Neil and Ian see:
https://www.acorn-as.com/

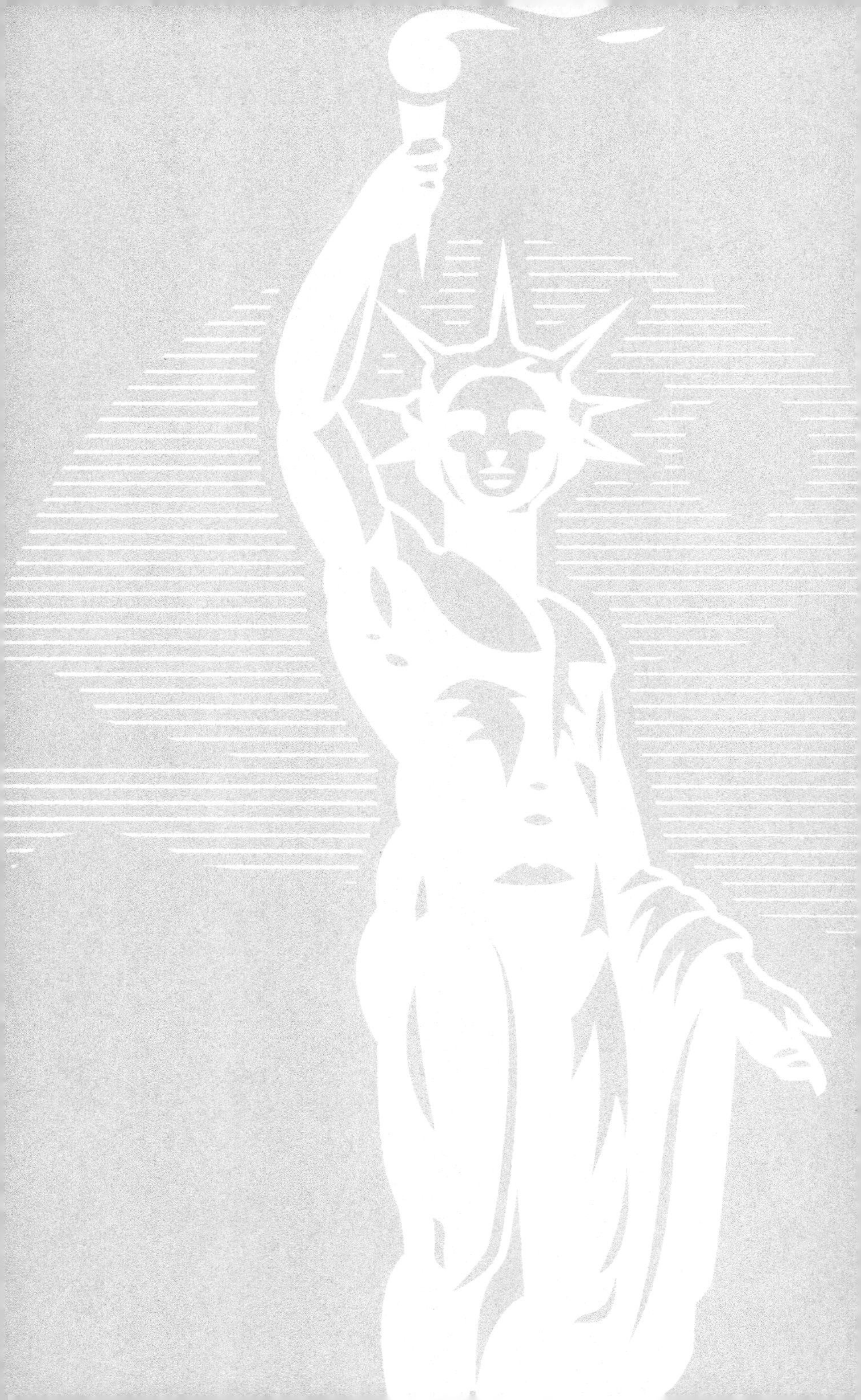

PART 3

THE UNIVERSAL IRON LAWS OF
FREEDOM

"Nobody Can Give You Freedom. Nobody Can Give You Equality Of Justice. If You Are A Man You Take It."

- Malcolm X

IRON LAW #10

Become Shamelessly Lazy In Order To Wildly Profit

There's a funny thing that happens when your back's up against the wall – male pride digs in and rather than asking for help, most just suffer in silence.

Plagued by the idea that it's beyond imaginable for anyone else, or anything else, to do what you do, like you do, and in a way that would make you happy.

A raw mix of pride, ego and the same dogged determination that allows any self-made man of value to stand on his own two feet in the first place.

An arsehole belief system that leads most to the resolution that when all's said and done it's always quicker, cheaper and more profitable to do everything yourself. EVEN though, deep down, you know you need another pair of hands just to help relieve the pressure.

Now for me, in my darkest hour, that mantra became a daily declaration of "I'll just…"

→ **I'll just do it myself this time…**

→ **I'll just do this one…**

→ **I'll just wait till next time…**

The trouble being that those fateful words, for too many men in this game, are just that – words. A crippling curse that leads to most drowning in a sea of overwhelm because every action, every task and every little thing, stops and starts with you.

And in my experience…

Freedom Is Impossible While Everything's Still Stuck in Your Head

→ You continue waking up at 2 a.m. (because ONLY YOU can remember what needs to done).

→ You continue to be pestered by customers (because ONLY YOU have the answers).

→ You continue to babysit employees (because ONLY YOU know what needs to happen next).

Or in other words, you will always continue to be the bottleneck and breakpoint.

A one-way ticket to No Man's Land and why now more than ever, ego must be sacrificed, and systems must be created. Because...

Systems Suck Shit Out of Your Head and Allow You to Pass the Buck

Now, when I say systems, think simple, step-by-step checklists. Nothing more, nothing less. Something that means you can immediately show someone else what you want them to do, step-by-step.

In fact, your number one priority should be the writing of checklists for all of the day-to-day shit and grunt work that you are currently doing yourself inside of your business.

The goal being to create the FREEDOM of being able to offload and outsource all of that shit elsewhere and off your plate.

What we call in this environment, the art and science of laser-focused laziness.

Because Systems Guarantee Consistent Action Without You Needing to Be Present (or Even in the Country)

Now in my experience, when it comes to creating systems like this, there are just three steps:

1. **Define the goal** – What is it that you need to get someone else to do? Think the goal or outcome of

the process:

2. **Brain dump** – Unleash on paper everything that needs to be executed in order to guarantee that the goal or outcome gets consistently actioned.

3. **Organise, prioritise and assemble** – Put everything in a logical step-by-step order that can be quickly and easily followed and checked off.

You see, when you start to systemise the shit that's in your head, not only do you pass ownership, deadlines and execution on to others but more importantly than that, you create FREEDOM in the ability to outsource and offload.

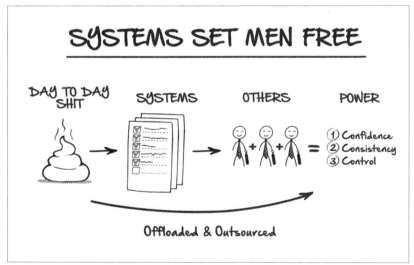

Case in point: Simeon Cattle, One Man Empire and the man at the helm of Project Shop – the UK's premier classic car restoration workshop.

A business that had quickly scaled, but was fast forcing Simeon into the bottleneck and breakpoint of all operations.

A situation that free-fell into a punishing plateau of persecution and panic if he ever dared step off the shop floor. The all too familiar story of responding to a self-inflicted barrage of shit, caused by keeping information, insight and intuition locked inside one man's head. Something often tolerated by even the smartest of men, thanks to the arsehole need of wanting to feel important.

Trouble being, just like many before him Simeon was starting to face the cold harsh reality that in the new economy he was now frantically having to earn money rather than print it. A self-administered coupe de grace, that was followed by a slump in sales as fires were put out and grunt work reigned supreme.

The Deckchair Technique

Now that said, he was smart enough to saddle up and get his head in the game.

The net result being that for three days straight he sat in a deckchair, on the workshop floor, just watching and writing.

Recording every major procedure, every major process and major action by putting pen to paper, as it happened and step by step.

Within seven days he had created twenty-seven paint-by-numbers systems for all major work done on cars and in the shop. Meaning that if someone now got sick, anyone could quickly and quietly step up to the plate and do what needed to be done, no questions asked.

A godsend, and saving grace when COVID-19 hit and the other hammer dropped – hard.

Because Simeon was free to finally remove himself from the equation, so that for the first time ever, and when he needed it the most, he was free from interruptions, free from questions and free from the day-to-day shit. Consider that, being 100% free to focus on whatever it took to keep the wheels of commerce turning and the money flowing – even in the middle of a pandemic.

The upshot being that despite the new economy and despite being in the middle of a global crisis, these systems started creating freedom and leverage, hand over fist. Unleashing a never seen before power that radically transformed monthly revenue from $30k to $60k, without the need for more staff or more babysitting.

A win-win and double whammy in anyone's books.

THE REVELATION FROM THE LAW

Man will not be judged by what he can do himself but by the promises of what he can coordinate and deliver. Remember the self-made man of value is in the game of buying and selling other people's labour and over-trading his time for clients' money.

You see, simple systems are the foundations that allow the self-made man to be in two places at once.

→ This is how you start building a REAL business.

➔ This is how you start building a SELLABLE asset.

➔ This is how you start to set yourself FREE.

It's why now more than ever, freedom will be the spoils for the self-made man who decides to systemise, because systems will always set men free.

IRON LAW #11

Automate Or Die

I've never felt more guilty or alone – quite frankly the noise was unbearable...

He just wouldn't stop crying, tears cascading down his face as another blood-curdling scream filled the ward at the hospital. Truth is, I was helpless as the doctor delivered the diagnosis I had been dreading.

You see if you rewind five hours, Barney and I were trampolining, and just ten minutes into the bounce, it happened. Barney shouted:

"Chase me, Dad!"

Needless to say I obliged, at full speed and full bore. A decision that was the catalyst for a scream like nothing I'd ever heard before. As I launched onto Barney's trampoline, he rolled under me, his leg bent double and a state of fear and panic flashed over his face.

Hence why we were in A&E and why I was getting the news that I'd just broken his leg.

Net result, for the next five days I was out of the business and out of my inbox making sure that he was OK. Funny thing was, on day six as I plugged back into the matrix here was the net damage to the business:

➜ **25 x new leads collected.**

➜ **3 x new sales appointments booked.**

➜ **2 x projects invoiced and paid.**

➜ **338 x follow-up emails sent out.**

In other words – ZERO IMPACT.

➜ **Customers were still paid.**

➜ **Leads were still generated.**

➜ **Prospects were still followed up.**

All without me lifting a finger.

The direct result of me choosing to ruthlessly Automate or Die. Something that started out of necessity and had fast become an addiction to removing myself from the day-to-day shit and grunt work inside of the business.

Because I don't know about you, but here's what I'd figured out the hard way...

Working Harder Is Not Scalable

In fact, if the law of No Man's Land has taught us anything it's that aimlessly pushing harder will always be the number one trigger of overstretch. And overstretch will always be the number one reason men like you and I are fucked.

And let's be honest. To-do lists are becoming filled with more and more, while time available is becoming less and less. Case in point:

The Day-To-Day Shit List For The Self-Made Man:

→ Follow up with customers, prospects, and partners.

→ Manage employees.

→ Respond to emails, calls and inquiries.

→ Check social media.

→ Talk to unhappy customers.

→ Send out invoices.

→ Track down payments.

➜ Search for more leads.

➜ Pay bills.

And that's just business as usual, before anything productive even gets started, considered or over the line.

It's why sooner rather than later most fall victim to the arsehole belief that bringing in employees must be the only answer. In fact, only last week I read this online, from a smart individual who I believe should know better:

"You don't have a REAL business until you have REAL employees and other REAL people in it..."

The fly in this statement's ointment?

Well, in my experience, REAL people are the number one reason why most REAL businesses can't efficiently scale.

Truth is...

Employees Are Not Scalable

You see right now in the 21st century, here's the trouble with relying on real people:

➜ They need sleep.

➜ They get sick.

➜ They can't multi-task.

➜ They make mistakes.

➜ They're inconsistent.

Now let me be clear, there will always be a time and a place for more boots on the ground. But subjecting others to the shit-show that most are currently operating with is a recipe for disaster.

In fact, if you have employees and you feel more overstretched than ever then this is the reason why. Because those that employee-up at the wrong time and without the right things in place end up even deeper down the rabbit hole.

Meaning most men at the helm of a business today would be wise to consider that the only scalable way to remove yourself from day to day grunt work, and for days at a time, is by deciding to let the machines rise.

You Must Automate or Die

Or in other words, put automated systems and processes in place that do the work of real employees without the backlash, backbite or babysitting.

As the new economy emerges, it's safe to say that every self-made man of value must start to consider there has never been a greater need for multiple things to be happening at once, on autopilot and at full force – without the need of manual input. It's the only way to remove the overstretch and relieve the pressure, for good.

Case in point: Do you remember this from earlier?

Right now, to become truly free, most would be wise to understand that it should start looking like:

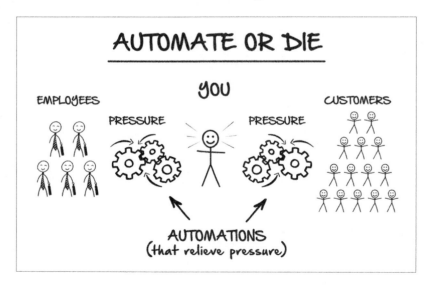

Meaning that you must start to...

Automate These Two Things First:

1) Your Follow-Up

That is, automating the communication with customers around the money-making part of the business – the three simple steps that convert prospects into profit:

Step 1 – The Warm-up Before The Sale

The automation of what happens on the run-up to any sales conversations or transactions, so you can consistently guarantee people are excited to give you money.

Step 2 – The On-boarding After The Sale

The automation of what happens after a sale is made, so you can consistently guarantee people are over the moon that they gave you money.

Step 3 – The Follow-Up After Delivery

The automation of what happens after your product or service has been delivered, so you can consistently guarantee people give you money again.

Or you could say the only three automations you will ever need for CONSISTENTLY turning prospects into profit.

When it comes to automated follow-up let me be clear. You must avoid the fear of customers catching you in the act.

You see, it's important to understand the fact that you know it's automated, I know it's automated, but the customer doesn't have a clue.

In fact, the customer just thinks you are efficient, reliable and consistent. Which of course is good news because efficiency, reliability and consistency with any customer are what build goodwill, and build it fast. And in my experience, goodwill is what keeps customers happy, and happy customers will always keep giving you money.

Which brings me on to what you must automate next:

2) Your Workflow/Delegation

Consider how you can take your simple checklists and systems and automatically put them into the hands of others.

Think:

→ Automatically delegating prospects to salespeople.

→ Automatically assigning work to others/outsourcers.

→ Automatically being sent notifications on what's happened and when.

Because the real power here comes from no longer having to rely on people.

While real people are shackled to real keyboards, you, my friend, will always be the victim of human error. Because I don't know about you, but in my experience humans (especially overstretched ones) are prone to make mistakes, and it seems that now more than ever it's little mistakes that create BIG problems.

It's why without automation you are 100% reliant on MANUAL checks, MANUAL reminders and MANUAL labour.

Now, let me anticipate the fallout from the arsehole belief that says:

B-U-T You Can't Automate My Business!

Let me be clear here. As part of this game, the goal is not to automate what the business delivers but to automate any and all manual grunt work that can be replicated or repeated.

Case in point: AJ "The Swinger Of Chisels" – One Man Empire and man at the helm of a leading traditional HANDMADE furniture business.

That's right, handmade.

Meaning his products are sold and specifically delivered based on the premise of ZERO machines.

Now AJ's first crack at the whip went to the wall, thanks to too much fire-fighting, grunt work and ensuing overstretch. Chances are, if you deal with the great unwashed masses you know the drill:

➔   Customers constantly chasing updates.

➔   Customers constantly changing demands.

➔   Employees   constantly   needing   babysitting.

It's the second time round, and when raising a Phoenix from the ashes he decided to stop the overstretch at all costs.

Now, the making of the furniture could never and will never be automated. But AJ became obsessed with automating everything else. Every time he had to do something manually he assessed how to automate it, so he could stop the fallout down the line.

Things like:

➜ Automating project updates with the customer.

➜ Automating the quote follow-up.

➜ Automating the post-delivery follow-up.

➜ Automating the sending out of "Thank You" cards and chocolates.

➜ Automating the answering of customer questions.

➜ Automating the delegation of tasks in the workshop.

➜ Automating the reporting of orders.

➜ Automating billing reminders.

→ And much, much more.

Meaning when all was said and done AJ had automated 1,278 manual tasks that needed to happen each and every month. That is 1,278 manual tasks that were now happening on autopilot, no matter what AJ was doing or where he was in the world.

Or in other words, in one fell swoop he'd he created 213 hours of FREEDOM every single month, simply by starting to automate.

THE REVELATION FROM THE LAW

Machine Is Always More Efficient (and Scalable) Than Man

This is about automating you, my friend, out of the daily grind, because there's a funny thing that happens when you automate your systems, your business and your processes and let the machines rise.

→ They never stop working.

→ They never let up.

→ They never get sick.

They just do the work, predictably and consistently, 24 hours a day, 7 days a week.

→ This, my friend, is consistency.

→ This, my friend, is control.

→ This, my friend, is your baptism into the art
    and science of passive profit production.

IRON LAW #12

Strategically Strike To Transform Weakness Into Wealth

A wise man once said:

"You can't build a house out of shit and expect it to stand in the rain."

It's the same reason that most men lose momentum inside this whole game, because they have no strategic plan, no strategic process and no strategic idea of how to continually build on what they've started.

The natural fallout of becoming a victim of aimless action. And one governed by the arsehole belief that if actions are ticked off a list somehow, things will just magically move forward. It's why...

Productivity Makes for Poor People

You see, productivity is a false prophecy and a road to ruin for far too many men. Mainly down to the fact that in most cases productivity is founded on lists. And the big problem with lists, especially to-do lists is that they only get bigger. Net result being that they force focus on more than one action at once – the kicker being that multitasking is not a male skillset.

In fact, if you've ever suffered from distraction, or been paralysed for weeks on end not knowing what to do next, then chances are productivity, to-do lists and multitasking is the reason why.

Productivity and to-do Lists Increase Overstretch. They Don't Stop It

It's why productivity plagues profitability and why when it comes to pushing past plateaus you and I must consider the only way to move forward is to stop days being dictated by aimless actions and instead have them governed by one strategic focus.

You see the only way to control the outcome is to only wage ONE strategic war, on ONE strategic front at ONE time.

Meaning right now all lists must be burnt to the ground with full effect and replaced with a state of mind and fundamental shift towards the light that asks the question:

What's the One Thing That, When Deployed Right Now, Will Move the Fucking Dial?

Because a divided front will always collapse into chaos, not conquest.

For a self-made man to be operating at optimum performance and output he must only be focused on ONE thing. It's the only way to continually increase power and control.

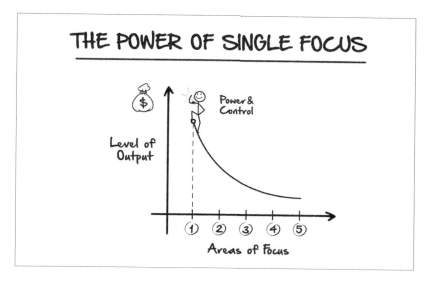

It's one thing to have a single strategic focus but it's another to deploy it with speed and full force. Trouble is, for most, the standard practice of a twelve-month cycle to get shit done is a dead-cat-bounce from the get-go. I mean twelve months, really?!!?

That's a long time to keep excited about one thing. And after all, a lot of shit can change in twelve weeks let alone twelve months. It's why as a man at the helm of a business in today's rapid pace of boom/bust, you must consider...

Now Is the Time to Start Operating in 90-day Strategic Strikes

In this new economy it's the only way to consistently keep pushing forward, without getting distracted or falling victim to the latest flux, trend or shift in the market. The fact is that 90 Days gives any man enough time to win one big war, but not so much time that boredom, distraction and disillusion sets in.

THE 90 DAY STRATEGIC STRIKE

Strategic Strike   Strategic Strike   Strategic Strike   Strategic Strike

The process is simple:

1. **Decide the War** – What is one thing that you need to deploy in the next 90 days to move the dial? Where do you want to be 90 days from now? If you were reading this 90 days from today, what would need to have happened for you to feel happy with your progress?

2. **Form a Plan of Attack** – What do you specifically need to do to win the war? What are the actions? Who is responsible? And what will be held to account?

3. **Allocate Battlegrounds** – For the next twelve weeks the battleground must be defined in advance. That means you plotting your plan of attack week by week, so you wake up every single Monday morning knowing what must be deployed.

For those that have never planned, an almighty force will emerge – the complete picture, an understanding, an exact and scientific battle plan for the next 90 days.

For those that have only ever operated in twelve-month cycles this becomes a declaration of war on deploying the strategies, tactics and systems that will guarantee that you move the dial faster and more efficiently than ever before inside of your business.

There is no greater sense of freedom greeting than just having one single focus.

This is how you stay ahead of the competition. This is how you stay ahead of the curve. This is how you keep momentum and stop the walls from crumbling down like a house of cards.

THE REVELATION FROM THE LAW

Control and power will always be the spoils for the man who refuses to wage multiple wars on multiple fronts. Because a divided front will always collapse into chaos, not conquest. Because everything else can and must wait. Only once a strategic war is won can other conquests be entertained or waged.

Funny things happen with this kind of mental focus, clarity and freedom – finally, shit gets deployed. And when shit gets deployed you, my friend, get the results, power and freedom that you deserve.

What Is True Freedom? How About Finally Being Able to Work Half the Time for Double the Money?

Meet the One Man Empire Who Finally Took Back Control of His Business by Leveraging the Universal Iron Laws of Freedom

As a devoted father of three, pillar of the local community and avid biker, Matt's time was already scarce.

You put on top of that trying to operate at the helm of your own business, in a down market, and you have a recipe for disaster.

A Quest For Freedom

Matt left the rat race some years earlier because he craved the time and freedom that standing on your own two feet offers. Yet five years in, he found himself at the helm of a company that wasn't growing. It demanded 14 hours a day of grunt work just to stop it from standing still or, even worse, go backwards.

"Overnight it seemed that more and more competitors were popping up from nowhere," recalled Matt. "Jobs that were a shoo-in just months before, were now shopping around on price looking for rock-bottom deals and bargain-basement prices," he continued.

Something made worse by the fact that if he actually won the work, customers seemed to be more demanding than ever. The all-too-common story of customers paying less and demanding more; picking his brain and posing problems at weekends, evenings and on a whim – precious time that meant Matt's youngest, James, was fast becoming side-lined and pushed out of the picture.

"I've never been more overstretched," remembers Matt. "I was literally one man stuck in the middle of everything. It's no wonder I was always disillusioned, distracted and downhearted."

Determined that enough was enough, Matt read about what some other smart, ambitious men were doing in their business with automation and by leveraging a NEW way.

The Power of the Strategic Strike

"That was my defining moment," explained Matt as he recalled his decision to start to automate or die trying. So there and then, he laid out his first 90 Day Strategic Strike with FREEDOM in mind.

"Up to that point, everything in the business was a shit show and revolved around me," he said. "So I literally took all the information that was in my head, put down on paper, and into lists. Lists of what needed to happen where, when and step by step. I guess you could say it was everything that I needed to do, to make sure that things happened consistently and like clockwork on every job."

Customers noticed the difference almost immediately.

"I had one customer that was blown away at the consistent quality – especially because at that time the business was just one man (me)."

Things then went from strength to strength as Matt set his sights on turning those checklists into little automations that happened without him having to lift a finger.

"I've never got so much done," said Matt. "In those 90 days I think I got more done than I'd usually get done in three, maybe four years. It's funny because 90 days seemed short enough for me to stay focused, but long enough for me to deploy some serious stuff!"

In one fell swoop and within just 90 days, he'd:

- Automated the follow-up after someone requested a quote.
- Automated the follow-up before a survey took place.
- Automated the follow-up after a survey happened.
- Automated the mail merging of documents for reports that needed writing.
- Automated the allocation of tasks when projects came in.

Automating Yourself Out of the Business (And Into Early Retirement)

145

It was an instant success, and eliminated 80% of Matt's day-to-day shit and grunt work almost overnight – something Matt hailed as "the ultimate freedom and like being retired!"

When asked how customers feel about all the automated processes, Matt laughed. "They don't have a clue. They think I'm manually doing all of it. I get people telling me all the time they are amazed how efficient I am. In fact, they actually thank me for following up! Little do they know that the email they think I sent was automated by a machine while I was asleep or out on the bike with James."

"The best part is that the phone calls and the pestering has all but stopped. Customers are automatically kept in the loop and because they know what's happening and where everything is they tend to leave me alone."

When quizzed about the new emerging economy Matt had this to say: "We've just had our best year ever, despite everything that's going on. Our competitors don't know what's hit them. Every time they get round to manually chasing up quotes, they're finding we've already pipped them to the post. Solely down to the fact that our automations are more efficient than any man will ever be."

Asked about what the future looks like, Matt simply chuckled. "Despite still being in lockdown, we've just taken on another employee and an even bigger office. The numbers this year are looking like they'll be DOUBLE last year, even though I'll probably work less than I've ever worked in my entire life. This kind of FREEDOM is exactly what I had in mind when I set up my business in the first place."

To read more about Matt see:
https://www.go-roavr.co.uk/

CONCLUSION

Your Invitation

OK, my friend, so by now – if you're like most other men that have set foot on this journey – chances are you are starting to see the light. A revelation and deep-rooted understanding that in order to take back control and be born free, overstretch must be stopped at all costs.

Consider these 12 Iron Laws as your guiding principles on the NEW way to play this game as a man at the helm of a business today. Your roadmap to start making more, providing more and being more as a man in this game today, without being bent over the barrel by an army of employees.

A battle plan to:

→ STOP The Overstretch.

→ STOP The Choke.

➔ STOP The Persecution.

➔ STOP The Persistence.

And get:

➔ More Wealth.

➔ More Power.

➔ More Loyalty.

➔ More Respect.

➔ And More Freedom.

That said, moving forward the most important weapons in your new armoury are the Rapid Deployment toolkits for each specific law. Meaning that once what you've read has sunk in and taken hold, I'd urge you to go back and do what needs to get done.

After all, if the pages inside this book have proved anything, it's that the spoils always go to the man who enters action with boldness.

So, What Should You Work on First?

Here's what I'd consider deploying as your Strategic Strike:

1. Define your rules of engagement.

2. List your daily standards, and do it quickly. There is no need to overcomplicate here.

3. Understand what your time is worth now and what it needs to be worth?

4. Figure out your first simple automation process. What can you automate today?

5. Wage War on your first weekly battleground.

Consider this book as the foundations for transforming your business into a One Man Empire. This is something that should regularly be studied, re-read, and then read again. Once you start holding yourself accountable and seeing the impact from the first couple of Laws, then move onto the next.

Join The Brotherhood

The tales from the trenches that you've seen first-hand, inside this book, are from some of the carefully assembled smart, ambitious men who decided to take the next step on this journey and secure a seat around the table of The One Man Empire Fellowship.

The transformations that these men have gone through, based on the Iron Laws outlined here, have been nothing short of life changing. This is one of my reasons for finally biting the bullet and putting pen to paper – so other men, like you, could start to make the same fundamental shift towards the light.

If you are interested in applying to take a seat of your own inside The Fellowship, then I invite you to apply to join me and the others. You can apply here:

https://ApplyForTheFellowship.com

After you complete your application, and if you are pre-approved, you will have the chance to schedule a conversation to see if you are a good fit for the room and the environment.

Thank you for deciding to join me on this journey and let's go punch this day square in the mouth.

Make More. Provide More. Be More.
Charlie Hutton

To the Men, Past and Present, of the One Man Empire Fellowship...

THE ONE MAN EMPIRE
MICROCAST

DO YOU SEE THE POWER IN THE IRON LAWS
THAT YOU'VE STARTED <u>UNLOCKING</u>

IN THIS BOOK?

If So, Then **Subscribe** To My FREE "One Man Empire" Microcast Where I Share More Iron Laws Of The Self Made Man Twice A Week.

You Can Subscribe For FREE

OneManEmpireMicrocast.com

STREAMING DAILY ON:

 Spotify  APPLE PODCASTS 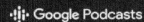 Google Podcasts

REFERENCES

Rhinehart, Luke. *The Book of Est.* Independently published. 2010

May, Rollo. *Man's Search for Himself, Chapter 7: Courage, The Virtue of Maturity,* (quote) Page 225, W. W. Norton & Company, New York. 1953

Robbins, Tony. *Awaken the Giant Within : How to Take Immediate Control of Your Mental, Emotional, Physical and Financial Destiny!* Simon & Schuster. 1992

Covey, Stephen. *The 7 Habits of Highly Effective People: Powerful Lessons in Personal Change.* Free Press. 1989

T, John. Rage Page: *A Journal for the Bad Days.* Independently published. 2018

Hill, Napoleon. *Think and Grow Rich.* The Ralston Society, Meriden. Conn. 1937

Hill, Napoleon. *Outwitting the Devil.* Official Publication of the Napoleon Hill Foundation. 1938

Hutton, Charlie and Hutchinson Emma. *The Orgasm Effect: The Business Owners Guide to Get Customers Screaming...Yes, Yes, YES!.* 2016

Dance, Charles. *'You Win or You Die' (2011)* Game Of Thrones, Season 1, Episode 7. Home Box Office. May 29, 2011

Stern, Howard. *The Howard Stern Show*. Originally broadcast on SiriusXM. 2014

Gerber, Michael. *The E-Myth Revisited: Why Most Small Businesses Don't Work and What to Do*. Harper Business. 2001

Mask, Clate. *Conquer the Chaos: How to Grow a Successful Small Business Without Going Crazy*. Wiley. 2010

Nightingale, Earl. *The Strangest Secret*. Laurenzana Press at Smashwords. 1957

Greene, Robert. *The 48 Laws Of Power (The Robert Greene Collection Book 1)*. Profile Books. 2010

Tomassi, Rollo. *The Rational Male*. Counterflow Media LLC. 2013

Suarez, Benjamin D. *7 Steps to Freedom II: How to Escape the American Rat Race*. Suarez Corporation Industries. 1994

Keller Gary. *The One Thing: The Surprisingly Simple Truth Behind Extraordinary Results: Achieve your goals with one of the world's bestselling success books*. John Murray Learning. 2014

Printed in Great Britain
by Amazon